Raising Girls

Raising Girls

Why girls are different – and how to help
them grow up happy and confident

Gisela Preuschoff

foreword by

Steve Biddulph

HarperThorsons
An Imprint of HarperCollins*Publishers*
77–85 Fulham Palace Road,
Hammersmith, London W6 8JB

The website address is: www.thorsonselement.com

and *HarperThorsons* are trademarks of
HarperCollins*Publishers* Ltd

First published in German as *Mädchen!* in 2003 by Beustverlag.
First published in English in 2004 in Australia and New Zealand
by Finch Publishing Pty Limited
This edition published in 2005 by HarperThorsons

11

A catalogue record of this book
is available from the British Library

ISBN-13 978-0-00-720485-4
ISBN-10 0- 00-720485-X

Printed and bound in Great Britain by
Clays Ltd, St Ives plc

This book is proudly printed on paper which contains wood
from well-managed forests, certified in accordance with
the rules of the Forest Stewardship Council.
For more information about FSC,
please visit www.fsc.org

Mixed Sources
Product group from well-managed
forests and other controlled sources
www.fsc.org Cert no. SW-COC-1806
© 1996 Forest Stewardship Council

FSC

CONTENTS

Foreword by Steve Biddulph

I remember the moment. It's not an easy memory: I am sitting in on the Caesarean delivery of our second child, terrified for my wife's safety, for my own powerlessness to help, and for this little life that is being prised out from the area that lies below the green surgical sheets. And then someone is saying, 'It's a girl!'

And amid the tears of relief are tears of joy, too, that catch me utterly by surprise. Our son is already seven years old; this new baby is long awaited. But had anyone asked me hours before, I would have given the old cliched answer – 'I don't care what sex it is, as long as its healthy.'

So why am I so happy? What had I been hiding from myself? A girl is something else – special to me as a man, wonderful in a different way from how a son is wonderful, and I will spend the rest of my life grappling with this, and happy to grapple, knowing it's one of life's gifts, a child who will become and then be a woman, and always, whatever happens, my daughter.

For a father, a daughter is something powerful. For a mother, equally so, but for quite different reasons, and we rarely feel this so intensely as in the moment they are born. And so we sit in this place halfway between feeling so lucky, so blessed, and so terrified about getting it wrong, and not being up to the job.

For help, we tap into one of the things that our culture does well – books, ideas, discussion, to help us broaden out our picture and learn from the lives of others. We don't have elders, we don't have a village to help us. But at least we have a questioning society that puts out so much chatter, and that brings us the thoughts from across the globe, that other people's lives have gone into making, all for us to digest, use or discard.

This book gets beneath the surface of you and me as parents of girls, because much of the trouble we still have with girls has its roots deep in our own experience, the wounded experience of growing up in a terrible century. Most of us, men and women, had odd and difficult times growing up: distant fathers did not teach us how to father, marital chaos and widespread divorce made us distrustful and unsure of how to form strong relationships and make them work. We had little in the way of spiritual depth: the old religions collapsed but only money and pleasure rushed in to replace them. We didn't really know the deep peace of the earth and sky around us, only the chatter of television and the clutter of bedrooms full of junk.

What we want to give our daughters, we often don't even have ourselves. But the search is on. A baby girl in our arms, soft skin, bright eyes, sharp intelligence wanting to grow and reach out, calls to us strongly to get our act together, to focus and go looking for the tools and understanding we will need.

This book is written by a woman on her own search, and has much that stirs up your thinking. Rather than giving you formulae, lists, bullet points and glib advice (the sure sign of a third-rate parenting 'expert') Gisela prods your deeper searching, so that things you have kept buried inside you come to the surface – beliefs, passions, forgotten memories that can help you and direct you to be a more wide awake, fully alive human being rather than some functionary who provides meals, drives the school taxi, checks off the school bags contents for another rat race day. What our kids will remember, and what will strengthen them, is the moments of closeness, honesty, and peaceful times that we spend in amid the scramble of life: the parts that we fence off and make special, where we refuse to dance to the commercial world's tune, and build a garden for love to grow.

Things have got better for girls. We need to remember that. There is a 'Sooty' video we found many years ago in a garage sale, that we enjoyed at the same time as being rather appalled when we watched it, and quietly put away on a high shelf. The compere gets children from the audience to come up on stage, asks them what they want to be. The boy will be a soccer hero. The girl will be a typist. Another boy a doctor. Another girl a nurse. This is progressive stuff – the girls actually want jobs! Twentieth-century culture crippled girls with narrow role possibilities, just as it crippled boys with inane pressure to be the brave soldier, the aloof father, the home tyrant, the frustrated wage slave.

We had a revolution, and now girls can do anything they want to, though it's turning out to not be that simple. The empire struck back, and ugly forces of commercial greed rushed into the vacuum created by the collapse of old values, and created for girls a whole new slavery: you have to be slender. You have to have big breasts (even if it means cutting your chest open and sliding in slabs of silicone instead). You have to work your whole life long, even if you simply long for some peace and quiet with your new baby, or to be creative, or have some time to just be. You have to have it all.

We've made progress with girls, but as this excellent book points out, we have a long way still to go. And some quite new directions, promising and world changing, just as the changes of the sixties were world changing.

For instance, there is a lot being learned about girls:

- That the apparently quiet time, the first year or so of life, is one of such rapid brain growth that everything important seems to be getting into place inside that little head and heart. The ability to love, to feel safe and relaxed, the ability to connect with another human being in empathy and trust – all happen in this first year, and we must not rush or abandon our daughter as if she were just a blob to be fed and stopped from crying.
- That the world we live in is very toxic to young children – the messages the media send, and the food on the supermarket shelves – so we have to show great care in what we put into her body, and her mind.
- That we parents also have plenty of cultural and psychological baggage and wounds that we can so easily pass on. I don't want to scare you here, but simply to remind you that half of what we give our children is our own selves, and these need much rehabilitation.

What else have we learned?

- That the twentieth-century idea of the father as the distant breadwinner, or the jokey stranger, has done enormous harm. We now know that fathers play an irreplaceable part in the confidence and self-esteem building of girls, a delicate role involving affection without invasion, fun with firmness, and care with strengthening levels of trust and freedom. Research into everything from anorexia to career choice, from sexual safety to educational opportunity, shows that a loving, involved dad makes a world of difference.

- That the rush to equality has caused much harm – through mistaking equality for sameness. Boys and girls grow differently, and should not be lumped together and expected to thrive. In secondary schools, especially, there are important reasons for separating girls from boys into classrooms where both sexes can be free from vulnerability to and pressure from the opposite sex; and free to learn and explore their fragile new identities without falling into the stereotypical and defensive pretence of being macho or sexy, cute or coy, aggressive or smart.

Your daughter may be a newborn. She may be a toddler, or a little school child. She may be a teenager, vulnerable but with growing identity and selfhood. She may be a young woman, relating to men, making her own way in the world, needing you less and less, or so it seems. She may even be a mother herself, coming to you with a new sense of awareness of the linkages you share. Your parenthood never ends.

The more you are awake, alive, and thinking and feeling deep into your own life – instead of zipping and rushing over its surface like a bug on a lake – the more you will have to give your daughter, and the more you will have to smile about as the seasons of both your lives pass by.

Steve Biddulph

Introduction

I would like to stimulate you to reflect with this book. What is really special about having a girl as a child? What kind of woman would you like your daughter to grow into? How important this consideration really is can be illustrated by the following story. Someone dressed a group of male and female babies in pink and light blue jumpsuits and then asked a group of dads to describe the children. They clearly treated the pink ones differently from the light blue ones. The pink babies were described as fragile, pretty, sweet and cute, although there were boys among them; in contrast, the 'light blue' ones were described as healthy, sturdy, strong and attentive – several girls also being among them.

People react differently to a male baby than to a female one. And that's quite normal, for there are of course differences. These are not only biologically conditioned but are based on social influences, expectations and premises – there has always been something like a girl culture or a culture of the feminine in all cultures and at all times. We can resist it, but never quite withdraw from it.

Only when, as parents, we become aware of which images and ideas of femininity we carry inside us, and which of these images are socially effective, can we take a critical look at them, perhaps argue about them and take new paths or turn back onto the well-established paths.

What do you want for your daughter? From what age is she to become a girl? How many months or years old will she be before she wears her first necklace? And when should her ears be pierced? Some parents have very definite ideas about this, and no-one will be able to dissuade them. Others have not thought about it at all, but probably carry unconscious notions around with them.

However, one thing should remain clear from the start: children are not putty in our hands. They belong to themselves and bring their own personality and unique 'life's work' into the world. As their parents, we are lucky to be allowed to accompany them for a while. In order for this to be successful, it's also important that we understand our roles as mother and father.

Each child is, in my eyes, a wonderful, unique gift. But individual differences notwithstanding, there are recognisable differences between the sexes. Women, for example, have more acute hearing than men and can better distinguish high tones – the frequencies that babies are known to use to cry. After just a week, female infants can distinguish their mother's voice and the crying of another baby located in the same room, from other noises. Boys cannot do this.[1] Moreover, women perceive visual detail better – a skill that is of great significance in a toddler's environment.

These days, new research is revealing important differences between girls and boys, men and women. Are these biologically inherited or socially conditioned?

I believe that parents of a girl should pay special attention to their own internal images of girls. They should ask themselves, 'What does it mean to me that it's a girl?'

This is very important, as it can help parents avoid burdening the child and her future life with a hidden agenda, for example, by saying, 'She should on no account become like my mother' or, 'She's not allowed to become as pampered as my sister' or, 'She should assert herself.' If parents are quite clear in their minds about their internal images, they can choose to stick with them or to distance themselves from them. Their daughter then has the opportunity to later rebel against this expectation, or to consciously assume the role.

Whether you have a boy or a girl, apart from wishing for children who are born healthy, it does seem to make a difference. The decisive questions we should ask ourselves are, what do we conclude from the sex of our child, and how do we deal with this?

Even today, the question of 'boy or girl' still plays a significant role in family planning all round the world:

- According to surveys in Europe, more couples wish for a girl, not a boy, as their first child – maybe in the hope that daughters would be more likely to look after their ageing parents in later years.
- In China, parents may only have one child – and most prefer to have a boy. Girls are undesirable, and are terminated in many cases. In India infanticide of girls is common.

What is your idea of a girl? Were you planning for a girl? If so, why? If not, how did you feel when a baby daughter suddenly entered your life? These are important questions that have a large bearing on how you view your task of raising a girl. Answer these questions and compare your opinions with that of your partner as well as some close friends. They relate to a very important issue: projection. By that, I don't mean slide shows in the living room, but rather how we often project our own beliefs, attitudes and expectations on to others, often mistakenly. If you can become more aware of your ideas regarding these matters, you will be less likely to project your thoughts on to others, including your daughter.

If you find this exercise rewarding, try the following 'Self-awareness questions for parents' to really get you thinking!

Self-awareness questions for parents

Here are some questions for you to consider. They are about you as a child and you as a parent, and a few ask about your daughter. You might like to simply toss them around in your mind, or you might like to write your answers down for future reference (which I would recommend). If you write them down, do so somewhere safe and private. You and your child(ren)'s other parent should both answer the questions. Just ignore the gender words that don't apply to you. When you have answered all the questions and developed a relatively clear profile of yourself and your own childhood, talk about these things with your daughter if she is old enough. This conversation is likely to stay with you for many years to come.

Then

When you were a girl/boy, what did you look like?

What were your favourite clothes?

What toys did you have? What games did you play?

What was your personality as a child?

What did you like about being a girl/boy?

What did you find difficult about being a girl/boy?

What were you not allowed to do as a girl/boy?

What duties and chores did you have?

Who were your role models?

What was your dream?

What did you often imagine?

Which insulting comments can you still remember?

On which occasions were you especially sad?

On which occasions were you especially excited or thrilled?

Now

In which situations do you behave like a typical female/male?

Which qualities do you particularly like in girls?

Which qualities do you particularly like in boys?

Which qualities do you particularly like in your daughter?

What do you wish for your daughter?

Which aspects of her life are you happy about?

I hope that *Raising Girls* provides you with concrete guidelines on how to approach your daughter's upbringing. I have drawn on experiences with my own daughter, scientific findings and the experiences of parents derived from my own research and consulting work. I have thought of the little girl I once was, and all the girls and women I have known during my life.

Fathers and brothers also play a critical role in raising girls. The experiences a girl has with the male members of the family follow her all her life. A woman does not allow herself to be defined without a masculine counterpart (and, of course, the opposite also applies), just as there is no loud without soft, no light without dark and no large without small! And so there are no daughters without fathers, even when the latter – for whatever reason – live separately from their daughter and/or have completely broken off contact.

You have a girl – who has her own distinct personality – and it really matters to develop this gift in the true sense of the word. I would like to accompany you on this journey. My point is to emphasise dangers and to prevent them; but above all, I would like to reveal an excellent pathway to cooperation.

Apart from this, I would like this book to be a journey of discovery of your own roots and notions, during which you may recognise what opportunities the birth of a girl offers you personally.

Gisela Preuschoff

ONE

WHY GIRLS ARE DIFFERENT

All parents worry about their children. They want to do their best and do everything properly – or at least avoid big mistakes. These days, most parents' expectations of their son will be very similar to those they have of their daughter. They merely want their child to be strong – strong in the sense of being socially responsible, independent, somewhat assertive, clever and affectionate.

And they want their child to be able to handle all the tasks that she will confront in life.

We're all individuals …

Long before a baby sees the light of day, a film is playing in the minds of the parents-to-be; they imagine what their life with the baby will be like, and they often have fixed ideas about the qualities a boy and a girl will have. This is completely normal – it is fun, and it increases their joy in their child.

While she was pregnant with a girl, one woman wrote in her diary, 'I have the feeling that I could just pull the finished picture, which is a perfectly formed little figure inside me, out of a drawer. She has already been born, because my imagination has already shaped her; she's a beautiful, strong, self-confident, lively and intelligent creature.'[1] On the other hand, the father of this little girl imagined a lovely, sweet, affectionate little girl he could snuggle up to and cuddle.

Apart from these images, parents should try to remember that there are many prejudices with regard to the sexes, and that most children develop quite differently from what their parents imagined in their dreams. Girls are by no means always calm, loving and good, just as boys are not automatically wild, aggressive and intelligent. Each child is unique: each child brings a distinctive personality into the world, and each is also shaped by her or his environment.

Most women who know they are expecting a girl identify completely with the unborn child. They see the baby as a miniature version of themselves and feel a strong symbiosis with the child in their belly: 'We're the same – we want the same things and are interested in the same things.'

The biological part of the story

What do the biological facts say? In the first weeks of pregnancy, when women as a rule don't even know they are pregnant, male and female embryos are identical, because they have the basic structures of both male and female sexual organs. They are only distinguishable through their sex chromosomes (XY for boys and XX for girls). The X chromosome originates from the egg cell of the mother, and the father's sperm has either an X or a Y. If the egg is fertilised by an X sperm, it will be a girl; if not, it will be a boy. Most genes lie in the X chromosomes, of which there are around 2000, among them the intelligence gene. The reproductive genes romp around in the Y chromosomes.

Purely statistically, more boys than girls are conceived, but more male than female foetuses are miscarried or stillborn. No-one knows exactly why this is so. It is assumed that either male foetuses are more sensitive to harmful environmental factors, or the mother's immune system classifies the male foetus as foreign and tackles it, in error, as an 'enemy'. Could that also perhaps have something to do with the mother's thoughts?

In the sixth week of pregnancy, the male Y chromosome gives the command to form male gonads; the X chromosome of the developing baby girl only induces ovary development from the twelfth week. During the course of the pregnancy, ovaries and gonads excrete sex hormones, which are involved in the formation of physical characteristics and also influence future behaviour.

The 'male' sex hormones are called androgens, and include testosterone; the 'female' hormones are oestrogen and progesterone. I have placed these classifications in inverted commas because all these hormones occur in both the male and female organisms, though in differing quantities.

When psychologists talk about a woman's 'inner man' and about men's 'feminine side', that is exactly what they mean. We all have male and female parts in us, and it is sensible to use both!

If the embryo has enough androgens, a penis grows and the female sex organs waste away and disappear. A vagina, fallopian tubes and womb will grow in the female embryo, and the male sex organs will die off. The fallopian tubes of the female embryo already store 6–7 million eggs, but by the onset of puberty this number has fallen to 400,000. On the other hand, boys only produce sperm from puberty onwards.

Between the ears

With sexual differentiation, male and female embryo brains start to develop differently. The clearest distinction can be seen in the hypothalamus, the hormonal centre or 'relay station' of the front and middle brain. From here, numerous bodily functions – sexual arousal, hunger, thirst, feeling hot and cold, and fight or flight reactions – are regulated. Here there is also a pinhead-sized group of cells, the so-called 'third interstitial nucleus of the anterior hypothalamus'. It is thought that this area controls sexual desire. The size of this group of cells is identical for boys and girls when they are infants, but it begins to grow in boys from the age of ten; and by the onset of puberty, boys have two and a half times more nerve cells here than girls.

The most often debated difference between the male and female brain, however, concerns the band of nerve cells connecting the right and left cerebral hemispheres. This bridge, *corpus callosum*, is definitely larger in the female brain, and it may explain differences between male and female thought processes. Girls and women use both cerebral hemispheres simultaneously, while males use only one at a time.

It has also been proven that girls' left cerebral hemisphere matures more quickly than that of boys. As the speech centre lies in here, boys – as a rule – learn to speak later than girls. The right cerebral hemisphere, which is responsible for the solution of spatial–visual problems, develops later in girls, which is why young girls often have difficulty imagining objects from different perspectives and orienting themselves spatially.

Birth differences

As a rule, the birth of a boy lasts an average hour and a half longer than that of a girl, perhaps because boys have an average 5 percent greater body weight at birth than girls. If a girl seems very contented as an infant, for example, it might be because her birth went smoothly and she had no traumatic birth experiences. In 1987 in Finland, it was established that newborn boys had a 20 percent higher risk of low Apgar scores than girls (the Apgar system is an index developed by the American doctor, Virginia Apgar, which states a newborn's vital signs; measurements are taken of breathing, pulse, base colour, appearance, reflexes). Premature births, vulnerability to mental disturbances and infections, and likelihood of accidents are all distinctly lower with girls than with boys.[2] A girl's parents are lucky: female babies are tougher and more robust than boys. We can only speculate about all the factors that contribute to this imbalance, but we can say that cortisol – the stress hormone – and testosterone, which boys build up, heighten the vulnerability of the immune system in male infants.

Perhaps the fact that girls are more socially attuned after birth and maintain eye contact longer than boys is connected to this higher probability of good health for them. They also react more strongly to noises and to other people present in the room, cry less often and are pacified more easily.

Even during pregnancy, the female body is three weeks ahead of the male in terms of bone development. At birth, female babies are already four to six weeks ahead of boys developmentally. At puberty, most girls are clearly and visibly at least two years ahead of their male classmates in development – clearly, these differences began very early in the piece.

Developmental differences and their consequences

Female skin is significantly thinner than male skin and seems to want touching more. The hormone that releases the need to be touched is oxytocin.[3] It is no wonder that women, whose receptors are ten times more sensitive than men's, think it is so important to touch and hug their husbands, children and friends.

Parents speak more often to their female babies, which certainly could explain why girls seem to listen more attentively. As little girls maintain eye contact longer than boys, they 'demand' that their parents devote more time to them, smile at them and talk to them.

Every baby begins to distinguish women's voices from men's very early on. She knows her parents' voices from when she was in the womb. With this, a more detailed classification process begins: for example, a deep voice means coarser facial features and rougher skin. The baby is gathering information that, years later, moulds her image of 'masculine' and 'feminine'.

At the age of six months, little girls are already more independent than their male companions: they can occupy themselves happily with toys and can comfort themselves with their thumb or a muslin.

The most significant difference in the first months is the speed with which little girls mature. Their height and weight increase more quickly, and they cut their canine teeth earlier than boys.

At the age of seven months, little girls can roll from one side onto the other (and often they can crawl already), are very skilled in handling a spoon, can draw lines and can pull up a zip.

These developmental differences continue apace. At preschool age, girls' fine motor skills are significantly better developed. Girls also start speaking much sooner and have more self-control (see page 33).

Parents' expectations and behaviour

So there are distinct, biologically determined differences between boys and girls. These are strengthened or weakened by their parents' behaviour and the whole environment around them. It is intriguing to know that in experiments, people faced with a group of infants clothed in yellow jumpsuits could not tell whether the babies were boys or girls. Even though they said they could! As soon as they learned what sex a child was, however, they reacted to girls differently from boys.

One mother recorded in her diary – which deals with the first three years of her daughter's life (she was born at the start of the 1980s) – that one of her girlfriends said, on seeing the newborn baby girl, 'Katie will be able to twist men around her little finger.' And the mother herself was sure that 'to have a right to exist in this world of men, a woman must look good'.

Is this still true these days?

The pressure to be fashionable and beautiful has never been as great as it is today, and girls suffer more than boys if they don't conform. I shall return to this later. Almost everyone notices that parents dress and groom their little daughters particularly carefully, and how a girl's 'natural' predisposition to smarten herself up is welcomed and reinforced by adults.

Female researchers have observed that parents look after their small daughters more tenderly than their small sons. This may have to do with the widespread illusion that 'men' must be toughened up, or that they are not as sensitive in the first place. As we saw, males are less physically sensitive than females,[4] but how did this biological fact become extended to include emotional sensitivity?

Who you are is crucial

Sometimes we forget that everything depends on self-awareness. What kind of person am I? How do I behave? What kind of example am I setting for my child? (To help you answer these questions, refer back to the 'Self-awareness questions for parents' in the Introduction.) The better you know yourself and understand your own anxieties, feelings and desires, the less likely you are to force your children into a mould or transfer your anxieties to them. Which means that the most difficult part about raising children – whether they are boys or girls – is the work you have to do on yourself. When you have a daughter, you must ask yourself what it means to you personally to be part of a female child's upbringing, and what femininity means to you. You need to be honest here. Little children see through insincerity quickly. What does the subject of girls mean to you?

Barbie dolls, curls, horses, high heels, pink jumpers and little cotton dresses? Or wise women, witches, grandmothers, female presidents, astronauts and taxi drivers? Femininity has many facets these days. What do you understand by it?

Your ideas of femininity

The examples of femininity that are being shown to girls today range from world-famous models to anonymous humanitarian workers. What matters to you personally? If you are aware of which forms of femininity you respect, which sorts you actually live by, and what tolerance you have for other forms of femininity, you'll be able to more easily answer all the questions that arise as you bring up your daughter. For example, if you can, sit down with your daughter's father (or mother, if you are the father) and make a list – each of you should make your own list – of the qualities and skills you value positively in a woman. (If this scenario won't work for you, try to do it with a friend whose judgment and opinions you trust.) List all your images, expectations and value judgements! Do girls have to be good at mathematics? Assertive? Cuddly? What does a 'good girl' do? What does a 'bad girl' do? Are you supposed to make such a distinction at all? Is intelligence a positive female quality? How do you value being down-to-earth and the capacity for love? And how do intuition, empathy or sporting skills rate? How important to you are manual dexterity and good appearance? When you've finished, compare your lists.

While you won't be able to force your daughter to be the things that you have written down, the things you value – being technically talented, highly musical or talented at nursing, for example – it is important that you know how you think about girls and women. Your daughter will choose her own way, but your ideas and thoughts will also shape her in important ways.

The types of girls

Socially, there are two main girl types these days, and they are contradictory. One of them is strong, self-confident, able to deal with change and eager to perform; the other feels herself disadvantaged with boys, has a low level of self-confidence, and sees her prospects as narrow. Then there are girls and women who refuse to be slotted into one or the other group and are searching for their own position, their own path.

The last millennium was mainly shaped by men. However, women will increasingly have a say in our future. Women will participate more in world affairs – but in what ways might this happen? Can you imagine your daughter one day becoming Prime Minister or winning a Nobel Prize? Regardless of which path your daughter takes, she will belong to a generation of women who will work with men to determine the future of this world.

She will help weave the fabric of human history, either loudly or quietly. So what kind of future do you dream of and wish for your daughter? Will you tell her stories about it? In your opinion, how should women and men relate to each other in the future? Have you spoken to your daughter's other parent about this?

What makes girls the way they are?

Female behaviour is not only inherited from a girl's forebears, it is also learned, as every girl is born into a society where the relations between the sexes are already firmly established.

Moreover, each family has its own culture and history, which is part of society's history. For us women, our female antecedents are of special significance. But it's not only girls who need to understand their roots – all children need to! What do you personally know about your origins? Which religion, traditions, belief systems and behavioural patterns that are part of your family tradition have you adopted, and which have you discarded? For instance, do you come from a family for whom hard work has always been a top priority? Or maybe you come from an alcoholic family, and have inherited some of the baggage that goes with that. Your home life as a child might have been very happy and nurturing, or else quite strict and stressful. These are some examples of family behaviour patterns.

My own view

When I think about what I wish for women who are growing up in this millennium, I think of qualities that have to do with original femininity, values that have largely been lost. How can they be dredged up, re-invigorated so that they find a voice again?

I wish for empathy, cooperation, helpfulness, a sense of community, creativity, and for the power of imagination, intuition, wisdom …

The editor of a well-known parents' magazine recently told me that she'd love to be a mother – full-time. But she dares not say that aloud. She loves being at home and looking after her children, but when her girlfriends hear that, they think she's reactionary. Must we women have a career? Do we have to become like men, act like men?

For me, femininity is connected to life-giving forces. I don't mean that I believe all women must bear children. They can decide that for themselves! But I believe it's important that they devote themselves to life: that they give fiery speeches to the United Nations General Assembly against war and for justice and peace; that they resist violence; that they join groups that aim to preserve Nature and not participate in the destruction of our environment. We should make our daughters familiar with Nature in all its forms and teach them to respect life – and to acknowledge women's achievements in all areas.

Femininity, for me, means giving life, protecting it, going with it – and seeing it pass. It is about recognising that we are subject to a rhythm, being aware that death is a part of life, that time after time there must be a farewell and a new start. Let us show our daughters the moon. If we observe it closely, we'll know a little of what it's like to live on Earth.

This is my personal opinion, not the truth. Do what matches your nature and your convictions – but do it consciously, and in the knowledge that you are a role model. If you want your daughter to be a strong woman, she will need strong role models. Being strong means being in harmony with yourself, expressing yourself genuinely, asserting yourself, and being able to structure your own life. Being strong means bidding farewell to the victim's role and taking on responsibility for yourself. Whoever does not seize her own strength is helpless. You claim your identity through your actions.

What we occupy ourselves with every day moulds us. Which possibilities do you wish to give your daughter?

The first role models for a girl are her mother and father. If you are careful, alert, communicative and present, you can't do anything wrong.

In a nutshell

- Girls are different from boys, right from the start.
- Before we can think about how to raise our daughters, we have to know what we ourselves think about girls, women and femininity. Sometimes we also need to question that, and do some work to change our thought and behaviour patterns.
- Remember, other people will also have their own personal reactions to the news that you are soon to be – or already are – the parents of a baby girl. Be ready for some reactions you may not be comfortable with!
- Have a good look at the world today and take note of what women are now achieving and doing – all these things are possible for your daughter too.
- Newborn girls are different from newborn boys physically, and some of these differences become greater in the first few months of life: girls are likely to want to be touched more than boys; many can play independently and comfort themselves earlier than boys can; and they often crawl earlier than boys do.

Boy? Girl? Human!

When my wife was pregnant for the first time, we decided we didn't want to know the sex of our child ahead of the birth. We wanted the full-on experience of pregnancy – no tricks of technology, no advance warnings of whether our lives were about to turn a distinct shade of blue or pink. As the weeks passed, we had lots of fun speculating on the boy/girl question – how I would have a willing and long-term football-kicking partner if it were a boy, and how I would protect her innocence against all would-be suitors if it were a girl. The funniest part of all this is that when the wee one actually popped out of my wife's body, both wife and I were in a state of such transcendental awe that it took us a full minute (okay, maybe a little bit less) to get around to checking what baby's sex was. In those irreplaceable first few moments of life, we didn't care a jot about anything other than that our baby was there, out, with us at last. It was a girl.

When my wife got pregnant again, we decided to find out at the amniocentesis test and scan what the foetus' sex was. We wanted to do it differently this time, in order to have the complete experience – that is, once not knowing, once knowing. It was another girl.

We stopped at two, not wanting to push the envelope too far! In hindsight, that process of guessing during the first pregnancy was very special: it was the only time in my life that I might have been about to have a son. Now I have two daughters, and of course I can't imagine it being any other way. But the dreaming was good …

Leo

TWO

DEVELOPING YOUR RELATIONSHIP WITH YOUR NEW DAUGHTER

As soon as a child has been born, parents have a special task to perform: you must say goodbye to your 'dream child' and greet, accept and take on your real one – with her qualities, her appearance, her gender and her behaviours.

The first step

Step one is to forget your pre-birth expectations. This is particularly hard if the child you are holding in your arms is quite different from the one you expected. Charming babies who seem calm and satisfied from the beginning and look lovable have an easy time of it, even if they don't match their parents' dream.

A screamer, however, who comes into the world bald and bright red, and who gives the impression of not wanting to become friends with this world at all, presents all kinds of problems. All the fantasies and illusions you created after seeing wonderful baby photos in magazines come crashing down. Perhaps your child became a girl when she 'should' have been a boy, and perhaps she was born too early and is still in danger of being disabled – or is already. People can achieve and change a lot, but we certainly don't control everything.

Having said all that, it is also the case that many parents experience the opposite: they are overwhelmed by their own capacity to love. They had never expected that a little creature, their daughter, could inspire so much love. They are surprised by the primal, deep force that rolls over them like a huge wave whenever they look at their baby.

True bonding – the prerequisite for healthy development

This farewell to the dream child is the first task for brand-new parents. You can then discover what a treasure you have in your real child.

Your little girl is the way she is. She will grow all the better the more you love her. In concrete terms, that means, for the first few months, being there for her all the time – she needs you to give her skin contact, to caress her lovingly and massage her, to nurse her, talk to her, carry her around and sleep near her. Love is an action word, and in the first months with a baby, love is in fact a very strenuous activity. However, it is exactly this loving – and tiring! – behaviour that is the basis for a secure bond between you and your baby. And having a secure bond with her parents in the first few years of her life is a requirement for every mental and emotional stage of development she will move through.

The impact of the 'attachment theory'

John Bowlby investigated and observed war children and orphans in the 1950s and developed the so-called 'attachment theory' on the basis of this research. This theory states that children can only develop their skills optimally if they have a trusting, secure bond with at least one adult role model. Bowlby caused a worldwide sensation with his film about a 12-year-old girl who lived all alone in a hospital. We have him to thank for several things:

- the fact that mother and child are now rarely separated in the maternity ward;
- the fact that often parents can stay with their sick children in hospitals; and
- the fact that parents know how important a stable, close relationship with their child is.

Even premature babies grow with fewer problems if they feel skin contact and human touch. It is interesting – and wonderful – that newborns are equipped with numerous powers that enable them to make contact with others and then to form a bond. Most parents react intuitively to these signals, and in this way the bond of love is strengthened even more.

If you accept your child as she is, and if you look after her responsibly and give her total security by nestling her little body next to yours, you will be giving your child the stable base she needs for her development.

You cannot spoil a baby – it is innocent and defenceless and dependent on your care. If you give her everything she needs and wishes for, you are doing the absolute best thing for her. Our knowledge of the powers that babies have, right from birth, has grown dramatically over the last few years, but parents don't need to study any of this; all you need to do is observe your baby and give her what she wants. Just as the little girl in front of you feels an inner urge to grow and to acquire skills and knowledge, you as parents also have inborn skills to look after your child. Follow your instinct and intuition, and you will do the job properly.

The 'positive mother/father complex'

Psychologist Verena Kast calls this first, pleasant, close bond with the mother the 'positive mother complex'. There is also a corresponding 'positive father complex'. According to Swiss psychologist Carl Jung, a 'complex' arises from a meaningful interaction between two people. You probably know about the 'inferiority complex' that can develop when a person is systematically devalued by their environment. No person is worth 'less' than another, but when someone is told that they are a failure again and again, they eventually start to believe it. The opposite is also true.

Making her feel 'uplifted'

Girls who are shaped by a positive mother complex take their right to exist for granted, are creative and can 'live and let live'. They know about everyone's right to respect, to express physical and spiritual needs, to self-fulfilment, and to a fair share of worldly goods. They feel uplifted by life, and enjoy their bodies, food, sexuality and being alive.

These girls, like everyone, eventually need to loosen their close bond to their mother so that they can develop their own identity and unfold their own personality. This task faces them in puberty – unless their mother dies earlier or leaves the family.

The importance of the father

Because of this inevitable separation from the mother (which boys do earlier than girls), it's important for girls to also have their father present in their lives from the very beginning – so that they can develop a 'positive father complex'. If girls' early experience includes their father – or, if that's not possible, someone who is not their mother but who also cares for them – they will find it easier to detach themselves from the mother–child symbiosis, and they will learn that relationships have various shadings: that Mum and Dad treat them differently, and that each parent has their own characteristics.

What special things do fathers do?

Fathers react to their children's speech with speech, just like mothers do. But fathers differ in that they often prefer physically stimulating forms of play, clearly defined movements, and abrupt changes between active and passive phases of interaction. The play style of fathers is often more exciting than that of mothers, and is highly prized by children. There is a lot more detail on the importance of fathers in later chapters.

Little girls who have both parents in their lives from the start soon learn different relationship patterns, and to attach different expectations to different relationships. This makes it easier for them to get involved in new situations: they already have a broader range of reactions than if they are dependent on only one parent. While a little girl experiences her mother as the same as herself, her father radiates the fascination of the stranger (which is significant from the start!). Most very successful women have had fathers who brought them up to be independent and self-sufficient. These women remember their dads as intelligent, ambitious, energetic and tolerant.

Don't give her everything she wants

Many grown-up women have told me that it's difficult for them to say no. It's important to be able to say both yes and no in your family. If you accept other people, including your children, as individuals, you also accept that each of you can make personal choices and decisions – about all sorts of things.

If your daughter wants hot chocolate for breakfast and you have none, for instance, you'll have to tell her no. She'll be disappointed and, if she's small, she'll whinge, cry and demand hot chocolate loudly. How do you feel about this? Do you say to yourself, it's normal to be disappointed and to express disappointment verbally and demandingly? Or do you feel guilty about your daughter not having everything she wants? Do you get impatient and aggressive with her?

Check your responses in these situations and remind yourself that it's all right to refuse your child something. However, also remember that you must often say yes to your daughter, because a yes is always a positive for her development.

Many children live with a lot of rules that harm their development. They are not allowed to:

- play in puddles
- climb trees
- mess around in mud
- unpack the saucepan cupboard
- experiment with glue
- handle scissors
- stand at the stove and cook something for themselves ...

But these are all things that children actually should do.

Other children have no barriers, and they lose their orientation. When everything is allowed, children become deeply uncertain. Saying no to your daughter when she'd like to watch television or have a certain T-shirt doesn't hurt. On the contrary. You might say no to playing with her if you're weary and exhausted and need a break. Explain to her why you can't play with her just now and when you will have time to. But remember, you should also accept a no from your daughter if she does not wish to put on the red jumper or to play the flute for her aunt.

Try to be a family where no-one has to bend themselves out of shape to fit in with someone else. Everyone should be able to decide things for themselves.

Set a good example

Living with children means that you must constantly ask yourself, 'What's really important for me?' If you can answer this question, if you know your values and benchmarks, you can set priorities. This has an effect on your entire life, but especially on your family life.

What are your values?

To help you answer this question, here are a few more to get you thinking:

- Which is more important to you, financial independence or good relationships with others?
- Do you pursue your own dreams or tend to adhere to social conventions?
- If you had to compile your own 'Ten Family Commandments', what would they be?
- What types of memories do you want to look back on when you are old?
- How would you like to be remembered by others, including your children?

When my husband and I asked the participants in a seminar for couples to list their life values and compare them with their partners', there was a commotion. Even people who live with each other often have different values. And there are typical male and female values. Do not criticise your partner if your values seem very different – just seek out the common values. Talk about what a particular value means for you and listen to each other, without judging. If you both listed humour, you're already on track!

Your children judge you according to the example you set. You will not be credible if you are a chain smoker and yet demand that they maintain a health-conscious lifestyle. And if you like to play with your children, you won't have to explain that joy in living is important to you; your children will know that!

Honesty is a quality that adults often demand from their children but don't demonstrate themselves. Examine your conscience – when have you lied, and in what situations have you disowned your convictions? Your children will want to speak to you about this one day. In the wonderful book, *Racism Explained to my Daughter*, Tahar Ben Jelloun explains his values to his ten-year-old daughter, Meriem. Jelloun, a French writer of Moroccan descent, responds to his daughter's queries about racism at a time when European nations were exploring how to absorb – or not – people from their former colonies. Jelloun examines the social, political, economic, and psychological aspects of racism, touching on discrimination, religion, genetics, stereotyping, immigration and xenophobia. What he is really talking about is values. The book is easy to read and has been translated into more than a dozen languages. I strongly recommend it to all parents.

As long as you have children asking you questions, you will be challenged to reflect on your life and values. That in itself is important. Even if you hold a view on a particular issue that is completely different from your daughter's, she will remember the conversation the two of you had about it all her life, if you treat her with dignity and respect. And though she disagrees with you today, it doesn't mean she won't agree with you in five years.

Be a good role model

I repeat, children need role models, people who set an example for them. How do you speak about others? Is your boss 'an idiot', your neighbour 'a jerk', the driver in front of you 'a moron'?

Observe yourself and be honest with yourself and your children, and that's how they will be.

A person who honestly expresses an opinion and stands up for their personal truth will always be respected.

A role model in action

Once, before my husband and I had children, a friend visited us unannounced, with his daughter, Anne. This was in the 1970s, before punks. Anne was wearing a shredded, 'graffitied' pair of jeans and a provocative top, and had brightly dyed hair – and probably a dog-collar as well, I don't really remember. Her father treated her with dignity and respect throughout the visit, though I knew that her appearance was not something he much liked. I admired him tremendously for this. Without saying anything, he clearly showed us all what tolerance is.

Eating with pleasure

Eating often becomes a tricky family issue. That's why I think it's important to give young parents hints on it.

Isn't it remarkable, in the truest sense of the word, that in our muddle-headed, mechanised world, it is our natural needs – such as eating, sleeping and sexuality – that give us so much trouble? Shouldn't it make us stop and think when, in a world of such surplus, so many people have an unhealthy diet and suffer from vitamin and mineral deficiencies? And why is it almost always girls who have eating disorders and are dissatisfied with their bodies in puberty? How does this all start – and how can we as parents stand by our daughters and help them?

The best nourishment in the first few months of any child's life is mother's milk. It is the food that was designed for us, and there is no equal alternative. From about the sixth month, children should also start eating some solids – carrot purée, for example. Then, once your child can sit in her own high chair with you at the table, you should start thinking about joint meals.

An important part of the 'culture' of every family is food – who cooks when, and with what ingredients. Of course you will have your own thoughts about this, but for the sake of the health of your child(ren), a couple of points are worth bearing in mind. Processed baby food cannot compete with freshly cooked vegetables in terms of nutrients – but then again, not all fresh vegetables are equally nutritious. Do you know if organic veggies are available close to where you live? Have you considered buying them? What about organic meat, and free-range eggs? Freshly prepared cereal, vegetables and fruit are the best food you can offer your child. Organic foods like these are grown naturally, free of chemicals and pesticides – whose long-term side effects are still not fully known – as well as genetic modification. This is the way the earth intended us to enjoy its produce. If, from the beginning, you avoid giving your daughter sugar (in the form of lollies, biscuits or fizzy drinks, for instance), you'll be doing a lot for her nutrition – and her teeth.

Moreover, this way you'll have your child eating almost everything you offer her. If she doesn't like a certain type of vegetable, don't be concerned. As long as your daughter hasn't got to know sugar and other processed foods (see below), she will choose what she needs out of the range of things you offer her. And remember, a healthy child also helps make her parents happy!

Limiting sweets

If you do not stock unhealthy foods in your home, no problems can arise. When your child comes into contact with sweets, stabilisers, emulsifiers and other harmful substances – in school, perhaps, or at friends' houses – she will be less vulnerable to such offerings if you've already laid the basis for good nutrition.

Parents have often disputed this with me, saying that their child will in fact go to neighbours' or friends' places to lay into the sweets there. First, if your child is still a toddler, she won't be going to a neighbour's house on her own, and will never be left alone there. So there is no reason why the adults there can't monitor what she eats. And if, when she's a bit older, she does eat sweets at her friends' homes, don't make a drama out of it. You've done your best, and that's enough – because that's all you can do. Anyway, if you look at the amount of sweet food your child eats in situations like this, it will almost always be the case that she eats less than her friend does. Children raised to eat healthy food do not, generally, choose to eat a lot of unhealthy food even when it is available.

When your child is in childcare or school, as well as giving her food to take with her, you can talk to the centre's staff and to other parents and ask for healthy food to be provided there. You may be successful with this. If you cannot get the centre or school to agree, at least you've shown your daughter how important healthy nutrition is to you. That helps her. And remember how important it is that your child knows your opinion, and sees that you know how to lead a happy life while following your own convictions.

How much food is enough?

Don't be too worried about whether your child eats too little or too much. A healthy child eats exactly as much as she needs. But note that this rule applies only if your child is fed an almost sugar-free diet. An excess of sugar leads to a desire for sweet things, and from there it's a slippery slope to deficient nutrition.

Food and power

If your daughter feels that she has power over you through her eating habits, she will exploit it. She'll say something like, 'I'm not eating that.' She knows that you care about this issue, and that her nutrition is very important to you, so she might think that you will immediately start to prepare something else for her. The result of this kind of exploitation is fairly common knowledge: processed food like fish fingers and tinned spaghetti will alternate on the table night after night, and if this sequence is broken even once, the little one will require serious persuasion to eat anything at all. Don't go down that path!

She can help you cook

Cook with pleasure, delight and love, and involve your daughter in the cooking. As soon as she's old enough, let her help choose what to cook, take her with you to the supermarket, help her learn to tell good-quality food from bad, and allow her to help you prepare meals. You can show a two-year-old daughter the proper use of a kitchen knife – as long as it's very blunt! These sensory experiences increase her interest in food and her familiarity with the taste and texture of different foods, and help to develop her intelligence.

In the first few years, children learn only through sensory experience – imitation, touching, playing, sucking and exploring things with their whole bodies. When you allow your daughter to be part of such a sensory activity as food preparation, she will receive just the stimulation she needs. And if you think about it, preparing and consuming food engages all five senses – sight, sound, smell, touch and, of course, taste – like few other activities.

On the other hand, if your daughter experiences mainly tinned or frozen food, she might reasonably assume that milk comes from a carton and carrots come from a freezer!

If both you and your partner are working, try to cook with your daughter on weekends and shop beforehand. If you live in the city, you could drive to the country now and then and visit a farm, so your daughter can see how vegetables are grown and harvested.

Don't be too concerned about whether your child is eating enough – every healthy child eats exactly as much as she needs

Mealtime behaviour

This is at least as important as your choice of food. Meals should take place in a friendly, peaceful atmosphere, if at all possible. Anything else is unhealthy. Don't criticise your child or partner during meals together, and don't argue. If problems need to be aired, go for a walk or sit in the living room and talk after the meal.

Find a quiet time to discuss with your partner what table manners you think are appropriate. Is your daughter allowed to leave the table when she has finished eating, or should she wait until everyone is finished? Can she play while she's eating? Can she serve herself at a certain age? If so, what age? And must she then eat everything she has put on her plate?

There are no fixed or right answers to these questions. You develop your own family culture by seeking answers together and emphasising the things that are important to you. In days gone by, for instance, a prayer was usually said before meals, children weren't permitted to speak at the table – unless spoken to – and everyone remained seated until everybody had finished eating. In many families, things have changed: these days there are some families who never sit down together for a meal.

What do you want for your family? How do you want to shape your family life in this respect? The moment your toddler sits at the family table, she learns something about food. What she learns is in your hands.

Important points about food for you and your daughter

- Meals with the whole family are fun.
- We should be grateful for our food – the amount and variety we have available are not things we should take for granted.
- Healthy nourishment keeps us well.
- Everyone can help with preparing meals.
- Children learn table manners most easily through example and praise – not through criticism.
- Everyone's body belongs to them – each person should therefore choose (from a healthy range of food) what and how much they eat.
- Fruit and vegetables should always be allowed as a snack.

In a nutshell

- Accept and bond with the baby girl you actually have, not the one you might have been anticipating.
- You are doing your daughter a favour when you say no to her for a good reason.
- Good role models are vital for a girl's healthy development.
- Your daughter is more likely to have positive, healthy attitudes to eating if you start her off with fresh, natural food and limited sweets.

Not tied to the apron strings!

Everybody was busy in the kitchen when I announced that, instead of receiving presents for Mothers' Day, I would not be cooking for three days over the Mothers' Day weekend. I wanted a rest.

There was a sudden silence. Everybody looked at me, and then my two boys – aged 18 and 15 – and their father turned to the youngest, Jesse – aged ten, and the only other female in the house – and said, 'Oh well, you'll be cooking for three days, then.'

Jesse threw herself onto the couch, put her feet up and announced, 'Sorry, I'm going to be a mother one day, so I need to rest now. I can't do the cooking.'

Then on Mothers' Day Jesse gave me a card she had made. It said:

Happy Mothers' Day, Mum
Please don't die until I get married
Love Jesse

I think she could see nothing but years of cooking for her brothers and father ahead of her.

Lisa

THREE

HER EARLY YEARS

In this chapter we will look at important areas of little girls' development, and see how parents can help this development. Again, the fundamental points here are that you should know what your own beliefs are, you should stick to them, and you should observe your daughter carefully and lovingly as often as possible so that you will know what she needs.

Language development

One area in which little girls are usually ahead of little boys is language development. According to one study, while girls can already speak three words at the age of ten months, boys the same age can only manage one.[1] At the age of eighteen months, half of all girls have a vocabulary of 56 words at their disposal, while half of all boys use only 28 words.

These differences also appear in their passive vocabulary (that is, the vocabulary they understand but do not use themselves). At sixteen months, half of all girls understand 206 words, while half of all boys are getting by with 134 words. Boys catch up to girls around the age of 20 months.

So overall, girls have greater language fluency: their left cerebral hemisphere is activated earlier, and this is where the language centre lies. This brings us back to the differences between the male and female brain. Interestingly, parents tend to respond to this difference quite unconsciously, encouraging their daughters' speech habits more strongly than their sons'. An American investigation showed that the number of words parents direct to their child – in other words, the amount of communication they initiate – gives a fairly precise prediction of a child's intelligence, academic success and social skills.[2] The more words, the greater the child's ability in these areas.

Without a doubt, speaking stimulates the brain and assists in building connections that are indispensable to a child's intelligence, creativity and adaptability. The language acquisition phase is therefore shaped by interaction – a link that becomes far more noticeable during the following years.

One language or two?

If you are in a position to bring up your child bilingually, do it. Young children are able to acquire language very easily and naturally in the first few years of life – and it is never again so easy for them. This ability not only leads to an improvement in your child's competency in her first language, it also has a positive effect on her overall intelligence.

Various studies have shown that both male and female teachers at preschool treat girls differently from boys.[3] Girls are frequently supported in their language efforts; their natural talent in this area is fostered. And remember, language stimulation takes place via speaking to children – not through playing cassettes, CDs or videos for them. Infants only improve their communication skills when they get live spoken feedback.

Parents usually do plenty of language stimulation as well – by talking to their baby, explaining to her everything they do, singing to her, and (later) reading to her. If you do not do this, your child's development will stall – this can happen, for instance, with children whose parents are deaf – if another person does not take on this role.

What do sport, music and mud have to do with intelligence?

Just like boys, newborn girls are equipped with 100 billion nerve cells, of which only a small proportion are already linked up to follow genetically specified circuits. The remainder wait for a meaningful learning program. Via sensory perception and motor activity, the nervous system builds neurological pathways that lead to movements becoming first acquired and finally automated. We can observe these connections very clearly in infants.

Steps in physical skills

At three months of age, a baby starts to watch her hands, and learns to guide them to her mouth. These are her first deliberate movements – hand to mouth. By frequent repetition, a pathway is formed; later, the movement is performed unconsciously.

In the fifth month, a baby will learn to reach for an object purposefully. The sensations coming from an object are transferred via nerve cells and electric impulses directly to her brain. Then impulses travel on from her brain to her muscles, enabling a deliberate movement. While your child is touching an object, she is noting the differences between its form, texture, colour and material and those of other objects, and in this way she is developing abstract concepts such as 'ball', 'Mum' and 'car'.

In the toddler stage, all a child's learning takes place via concrete, sensory perception. So give your daughter various materials to feel: something smooth, something soft, something hard, something light … above all, let her play a lot with mud, sand and water, and experiment with several different kinds of movement.

By the way, if your daughter plays the piano, all parts of her brain will be activated. Music, sport, painting and moulding soft materials aren't just for fun; they also foster general intelligence – assuming, of course, that your daughter devotes herself voluntarily and happily to these activities.

Talking and listening to your daughter is the best way to help her improve her language skills

Goodbye nappies, hello potty

Most little girls get rid of their nappies quickly and easily. If she is interested, take your daughter with you when you go to the toilet. Show her what you do there and offer her the chance to copy you – with the help of a toilet-seat or potty.

I recommend that you take off her nappy in summer, so that she will notice when wee-wee comes. Don't apply any pressure. Be glad with every success and don't pay the whole operation too much attention. Sooner or later, every child is toilet-trained.

When toilet-training seems not to be working

Parents need to be sure about one thing: if children have problems getting rid of their nappies, it never has anything to do with annoying or punishing their parents. Rather, it is because they misunderstand something or are worried or frightened about what's going on. Patience, sympathy and understanding are what children need during this time. Punishment, disdain or laughing at them will only lead to a shift in or an intensifying of the problem. Then it will be more and more difficult to find a solution.

Girls learn earlier

Author Susan Gilbert maintains that one of the main differences between boys and girls is that girls learn more easily from their mistakes.[4] Do you agree?

An American psychologist, Eleanor Maccoby, observed one-year-old boys and girls in a doctor's waiting room.[5] While the boys often grabbed at things their parents had forbidden, the girls generally stuck to the rules. Were the girls simply better behaved?

There's a classic experiment to test the memory skills and impulse control of eight-month-old crawling children. An object is hidden in one place, and the child is allowed to find it; then, while the child is watching, it is taken and placed somewhere else. Most children will initially look where it was hidden the first time. Either they have forgotten that it has been moved to a new place or they cannot resist the impulse to look for it where they previously found it. In one study, the older they were, the better both girls and boys became at this experiment, but girls made faster progress.

The situation is similar with toilet hygiene. Most parents notice that girls control their bladders earlier than boys do. One investigation found that at two-and-a-half years old, 30 percent of girls and only 15 percent of boys were toilet-trained.[6] By the age of three, 70 percent of girls had managed it, but only half the boys had. Maccoby traces this difference back to the variation in degree of brain maturity in boys and girls of the same age. Of course, you will know of exceptions to these generalisations.

All in all, girls generally seem to be able to control themselves better than boys. This is also apparent in terms of tantrums, which are normal for one- and two-year-old girls and boys. From the age of three, however, girls have fewer tantrums than boys. They also tend to adjust to preschool life more smoothly than boys.

Sexual curiosity

While a little boy's penis is clearly visible and is, quite early on, discovered to be a source of pleasure, it's not so straightforward with girls. Parents of girls sometimes forget that their daughter also feels sexual desire, so when girls experiment with their sexual organs, adults will often forbid it or feel that it is somehow risky.

Little girls discover this wonderful body part early, all by themselves – and we should simply let them do so. Girls who are allowed to explore their own body in a casual way are not likely to feel penis envy. And by the way, girls can pee standing up, too. Parenting author Marianne Grabrucker writes that she used to put a smock – and no underpants – on her little daughter in summer. The little one could then pee outdoors at any time, whether squatting or standing.

Every person's body is a miracle – our daughters should know this about themselves before the media and advertising teach them about the type of body 'preferred' in Western society. And what distinguishes a woman's body from a man's is its capacity to carry new life, to bear a child. That is what confers esteem and respect on it, not how closely it resembles an hourglass!

Fathers and daughters – what's okay?

Many fathers are uncertain about how to behave physically around their daughters, because of the possibility of false accusations of sexual impropriety. What can fathers do with their daughters and what is forbidden? There is a very simple rule from family therapy that always applies: keep the generation gap at all times. As an adult, it is your duty and responsibility to set limits. Adults always bear responsibility for the child, because they have greater life experience and are in every respect the 'stronger' party

As long as you, the father, have a high regard for your daughter and respect her personality, and know yourself well – with all your strengths and weaknesses – then there is little chance of any inappropriate physical behaviour occuring between the two of you. Just keep the generation gap, and go on spoiling your daughter with tenderness.

Organise your life to provide the maximum fulfilment – including job and career, if they are part of what fulfils you

Do you want to return to work?

In the developed world working parents – and especially mothers – have it anything but easy. Often when mothers take on positions of responsibility in organisations, people ask them, 'How will this affect your children?' But a man in the same situation would not be asked this. Because this is how society still works, I will address this section to mums – but that does not mean I assume dads won't take time off work, or don't want to do so.

Regardless of the childcare centre arrangements and restrictions that exist where you live, we should first ask, is it sensible to go to work if you're a mother with a child under the age of five? How does your child feel about it?

There are several things to consider. Do you want to work again? Do you have to for financial reasons, or is it that you don't want to be thought of as an unemancipated housewife? Do you get a lot of pleasure from your work outside home? Or would you rather be with your child? And if you do want to work again – what working hours would suit you?

First, remember the rule: happy parents are likely to have happy children. If you're dissatisfied as a mother, this will filter through to your child. You'll have seen this yourself in your daily routine. So if you are a woman who loves your job, and when you're at home you feel chained to your daughter like a slave, do something about it. It's more sensible to look for a qualified carer for your daughter, someone who will look after her happily, than to sit at home howling into the baby food or ready to strangle the nappies in anger. It is definitely not natural, in the true sense of the word, to spend many hours in isolated mother–baby togetherness at home. Originally, it was always a group of women who minded and fed the children – and who at the same time also did other important domestic jobs. That set-up relieved individual mothers and gave the children space for new experiences and social learning. There was always someone there to comfort a child and play with her; and in the case of a crisis, Mum was always nearby.

More and more women are raising children alone. Most of them have to be working mothers, whether they want to or not, simply to manage financially. Whether you work because you want to or because you have to, your working life will not harm your daughter if you get her accustomed to one contact person who takes care of her lovingly and consistently.

Childcare options

If you think (or know) that you may need childcare at some stage, you might need to put your name down at a number of childcare centres early on – these days, that might mean before your baby is born! But at whatever stage you check out child-care facilities, make a list of things you think the centre should be doing before you go and then look carefully to see if it matches these expectations. Some general, initial questions to consider include: what kind of impression do the children there make on you? Do they seem happy and busy? How do the childcare workers deal with the children? Would you like to be a child in such a facility yourself?

If you decide against using a childcare centre, family day care – a relatively small number of children (say, five or six) cared for in a private home – is another option. Or a reliable baby-sitter at your own home (we can call her a 'day mother') may be a good alternative. She should come to your place, if at all possible, so you needn't tear your child out of her sleep and expose her to the daily hustle and bustle of working life. Of course this will be expensive, but if you are honest, you'll agree that a really good mother-substitute is worth a decent pay packet. Before you employ someone, watch her and your daughter together closely for a while – and give both of them a bit of time to get to know each other. When the two of them have established a stable relationship, comparable to the one with a grandmother, aunt or uncle, then you can go to work with a clear conscience.

Of course, it would be wonderful if your daughter's father could look after her in your absence. However, there are several factors that combine to make this difficult:

- Many fathers do not want to give up their job and stay at home with the children.
- There may not be many part-time jobs available for those who would be happy to reduce their working hours.
- Most men earn more than their partners, so many families can't afford to have the father stop work.

And in many cases, the family's financial situation means that none of these possibilities can realistically even be considered. This is a great pity, because it perpetuates the 'fatherless society', which may continue into future generations.

Another difficulty that many parents face today is the fact that they only see each other for a few hours a day, which means that they really have to make an effort not to let their own relationship suffer.

Many women would gladly work from home – and in some occupations that is already possible, thanks to modern technology. It sounds good, and if you are able to determine (and control) how much you work, and can make and keep to your own rules about work time and family time, this may be a solution. However, if you work from home and can't establish such limits, first you and your daughter will suffer, and then the whole family will suffer. Your daughter will suffer because she gets too little stimulation and has no playmates; you will suffer because you don't finish your work due to too many interruptions; and your family will suffer because there is no clear distinction made between work and family life, and they become blended.

Choosing to stay at home

If you are a woman who is gladly interrupting your working life for a while in order to be there full-time for your family, stick to your guns and enjoy this period of your life! You'll find there are lots of ways you can be creatively active: you can cook, make toys, sew clothes, decorate your living space lovingly, write, paint, take photographs, or spend time on a hobby that fulfils you. You may make friends with people nearby who also have young children. You'll also enjoy being with your child and observing her progress as she develops. Don't let yourself be talked into believing that you're old-fashioned or that you're putting your career at risk – countless other women are doing exactly the same as you.

It is simply wonderful to live with a child! Just listen to Steve Biddulph, the well-known Australian family therapist, who speaks out vehemently against strangers looking after your child. His credo is, 'Why did you have the child if you are just going to have her looked after by strangers? Are we living in a cuckoo society where you place your young in someone else's nest?'[7]

Money isn't the only factor

Most people's way of life is determined largely by their economic obligations, but it would be unfair to blame all the problems of children and families on the fact that many mothers have to work. (By the way, the materialistic approach of our society is by no means without alternatives, and we all bear responsibility for our lifestyle, whether we have children or not.) Ill-treatment and neglect can occur when mothers are at home, especially when they are being stretched too far and cannot properly manage their duties. One of the childcare options outlined above would be the salvation of many of the children in such families. We must ask ourselves what kind of culture it is that drives parents to such extremes. If we compare our life with that of people in the Trobriand Islands (in Papua New Guinea), for example, we'll quickly find the answer. We are paying a high price for our so-called 'civilisation'.

On the other hand, you as parents carry the seed of a new culture within you. Your children are your future. Which skills do they need? And in what frameworks will they best develop these skills?

I would like to give you a piece of advice. Make the decision about whether or not to go back to work by following your heart, if your financial situation allows it. Think about how you would organise your life, if you could, to derive the maximum satisfaction from it. What would this life look like? Leave all the arguments to one side and just contemplate this imaginary, ideal life. Write down the elements that make up this life, or draw a diagram of it if that feels more natural to you. Shift yourself mentally into this life – does it work? Is it what you want?

Now sit down with whoever you want to involve, discuss this life, and try to work out how to make it come true, step by step. Barbara Sher's book, *Wishcraft* (see the bibliography) may help you with this.

My own vision

I dream of conquering isolation by living more of a communal life. In this dream, young families live very close together and support each other. Children play together, and parents are freed from the isolation of the nuclear family. The tasks around the home and grounds are taken care of jointly. Some mothers and fathers work outside this community, while others look after the children. Some singles and couples without children also belong to this extended group, and take on tasks they enjoy. There are surrogate grandparents and godparents. Conflicts are constructively solved, and the children all have several role models, thereby learning about various lifestyles and value systems. Every person contributes his or her own skills and receives help if required. Humanity is a key issue in this scenario.

In a nutshell

- As babies and toddlers, girls develop faster than boys physically, emotionally and intellectually.
- Let your daughter explore her body naturally and without restriction.
- With fathers and daughters – as with parents and children generally – it is vital to 'keep the generation gap' at all times.
- In considering whether or when to return to work, bear in mind that happy parents are more likely to have happy children.

Up close and too personal

My daughter, Katie, and I were at the Chiang Mai Zoo, in northern Thailand, peering over the cement wall into the elephant enclosure. Katie was about two years old, and I was holding her in my right arm, waving a banana with the left hand at the elephant inside. The elephant mosied over to the wall – unlike in Western zoos, where there's no feeding of the animals, at the Chiang Mai Zoo vendors sold bags of peanuts and stalks of bananas especially for that purpose.

I gave her – I'm certain it was a female – a banana, which she delicately inserted into the envelope of her mouth. Then her trunk reached across the wall for more. I had more, but first I wanted to check out that extraordinary trunk. It was like a big tentacle, with little bristly hairs, and lots and lots of wrinkles. I stroked it. I looked into the vacuum tube of its opening – a long, narrow tunnel. I gave it a little breath, a little tickle up the nose from me to her, and I tickled the outside of it a bit, too, marvelling at how elastic and strong it seemed, and wondering how long my new friend would accept my playfulness.

Not very long at all, as it turned out. Suddenly the trunk I'd been tickling reached out and wrapped its coiled strength around my left wrist. I waited a moment, then tried to draw my hand back a little bit. The elephant exerted her mighty pull precisely the same amount in her direction, with – and I could feel the vast energy behind it – plenty of power in reserve.

I stood there a moment thinking, 'I am in the complete grip of an immense force of nature, who is annoyed with me …', and I met Katie's gaze of quiet alarm. The elephant looked at Katie, too.

I wonder if she remembered once being a mother, imperfect as we all are. She released me.

'Give the elephant another banana?' Katie asked.

'Okay,' I breathed. I gave her the whole bunch.

Mindy

FOUR

HER EMOTIONAL WORLD

In the last two chapters we have looked at how to manage some of the most important 'external' matters in your life as the parent of a girl. I would now like to shift the focus to the internal world of your daughter, and especially to the vital and dynamic world of her emotions. First, let's look at how to help her feel good about herself, and how she can safeguard her inner life.

The importance of self-esteem

High self-esteem is the best protection you can give your daughter. High self-esteem means you consider yourself important and valuable, regardless of your appearance, ability or performance. If you feel you are important, you speak up for yourself and defend your rights and your body. Any woman can become the victim of a violent act, of course, but statistically speaking, the possibility is very slight – and, in the light of the research cited by Nicky Marone (see box, page 53), even slighter for women with high self-esteem.

As children, my friends and I often played the game, 'Who's afraid of the big bad wolf?' One group of children, standing in a row, would call that question out.

'No-one,' the other group would roar, facing them.

'And if he comes?'

'Then he just comes!'

At this point, you had to run – the aim was to get to the other team's area without being caught. Sadly, this game has gone out of fashion, but wherever girls played it, they made the same agreeable and exciting discovery: that you can take a risk, emerge victorious and get to your destination safely. If your daughter plays a team sport, she will experience something similar.

Allow your daughter to express all her feelings, even the really negative ones like jealousy, temper and rage. Aggression is not all bad, as it can help us stand up for ourselves and assert ourselves in life. We women are allowed to feel these emotions, and we ought to let them run free! In earlier times, girls were rarely allowed to defend themselves or to be loud or passionate. This was very detrimental, because expressing your true feelings is essential for good health. Teach your daughter that she can say 'no' and that she has the right to decide how to use her body. This concept extends even to little things like not persistently demanding a kiss from her if she is not so inclined; and not forcing her to sit on your lap if she doesn't want to at the time.

The risk of overprotectiveness

In education programs that I run for female educators, many parents tell me that they always drive their children where they need to go and pick them up from there later, because they're afraid that their children will be victims of sex offenders. While this is perfectly understandable and in many cases necessary, there may be some occasions when they could quite safely walk there and back or take public transport. The reality is that we can't protect our daughters from all the risks in the world, so we need to prepare them to go out without supervision. And one way we can do this is to teach them to scream, kick and defend themselves. Our inhibitions can sometimes put us in greater danger than would otherwise exist. To exemplify this, psychologist and author Nicky Marone quotes an investigation in which scientists filmed ordinary people, pedestrians in New York, as they strolled along the street.[1] This film was shown to a group of criminals, who were asked to say which people were worth considering as victims. The results were unequivocal: it was always the same people who were selected. They stood out because of their inhibited body language, which indicated fragility, uncertainty and a general lack of self-confidence.

The best way you can protect your daughter from fear, and from danger, is to ensure that she has good self-esteem. There are many ways to do this, and you can start from the moment she is born.

My own father

I had a very loving father, so I can tell you how I felt his love. He kept several of my child drawings and looked after them as if they were treasures. He often took me for a walk and would hold my hand; I can still feel that beautiful sensation today.

He read me fairytales and stories – and they are still with me. He showed and told me a lot about animals and plants, and I have remembered much of this. He allowed my little brother and me to stay quietly in his study while he sat at his desk working. That made us feel important. He sang songs to us and played with us – I can still see these scenes in my mind today.

Later, he tried helping me with maths exercises – in vain, I'm afraid. He typed up my school compositions and kept them. He went to see my teachers and talked with them for as long as was necessary. He was always ready to answer my questions, or to look up the answer if he didn't know. He tried to protect me from harm and always gave his opinion – often, unasked. I didn't always want to hear what he had to say: sometimes I rolled my eyes. Today, though, I know that in most things he was right.

Fathers and self-esteem

Fathers can do a lot for their daughter's self-esteem. When a daughter feels loved, respected and highly regarded by her father, she is getting much more than what would fit into an olden-day dowry box. Mind you, your daughter needs to be able to feel this love and respect from your behaviour – words are just 'empty noise' when they are not supported by deeds.

The father who tells his daughter she's fantastic, but at the same time asks why she only got a pass in English or why she didn't jump higher, may find that his words are not believed. Spend time with your daughter, give her recognition for what she has achieved and teach her the things that only you, as her father, can teach her. It doesn't matter what your particular skills are: whatever skills you have, I assure you, your daughter can use them!

Encourage her early and often

The chance to strengthen your daughter's self-esteem exists even when she is a toddler. Don't hurry to her aid if things go wrong – leave it to her to find solutions by herself, and possibly to 'fail' and try again. When she's stacking building blocks, for example, the tower will topple if it gets too high and is not stable. At some point, your daughter will learn how high a tower can be without falling down. (Incidentally, playing with building blocks also fosters her powers of spatial imagination.) It's also completely normal for toddlers to fall over when they learn to walk – let them fall and stand up again, as many times as it takes. These experiences are indispensable for little girls and little boys, as they strengthen their self-confidence and self-assurance.

Observe your daughter and find out what she's interested in and enjoys, and what she's good at. Support her in what gives her pleasure – and urge her to try out new things. But remember, no matter how much encouragement you give her, you won't make a daredevil out of a reserved child – and don't try to change a daredevil into a reserved child either, as that will be equally doomed to failure.

When she is little, your child will feel loved and valuable when you look after her in a consistent way, carry her often and touch her tenderly, and when you speak to her and listen to her and take her needs seriously. Children only develop self-esteem when they feel the unconditional love of their parents, a love that is founded on their worth as a human being, not on their appearance or performance.

This way, your daughter's self-esteem will grow even when she fails at something – or when she is not as cheerful as you'd hoped she would be, or when she doesn't perform well, or when she doesn't look the way you expected. It will grow as long as she feels, clearly, 'My parents love me – just the way I am!'

How does a child know that she is loved by her parents? By feeling that her parents look after her carefully, that they have time for her, show interest in what she does, and express their affection. It's really quite simple, isn't it? You just have to treat your child like your best friend: with respect and dignity. When your daughter draws her first line, praise her. Your joy is an incentive for her to continue, even to try something new – perhaps her first circle might appear soon! Every moment of such praise and support is a step in her development.

Let her imagine and create

Criticism, negative judgments, derogatory, ironic comments and ignorance are all harmful. Attacks on a child's self-esteem, which we often hear from adults – and even from teachers – can have disastrous long-term consequences. In this context, I'd like to stress that television harms small children. First, it stops them doing something active, and it is through doing things, being active, that self-esteem develops. Second, the flood of images from the television blocks out their inner pictures and reduces their fantasy and imaginative life. Imagination is the basis of all creative intelligence.

Fathers, daughters and play

In one study, fathers were asked to do jigsaw puzzles with their sons and daughters. If the little boys had a fit of temper because they couldn't do it, the fathers ignored it and continued working with them on a solution to the problem. But if the daughters started to cry, they were comforted with statements like, 'It doesn't matter, darling.' The daughters were often helped more, as well.

If little girls often have this kind of experience, in the long run they will make less of an effort with things – some will even behave as if they are helpless. Trying to make it easier for girls, and not letting them work on problems until they have solved them does not help build their self-esteem. Do with your daughter what you do (or would do) with your son – let her, in this case, try to figure out on her own how the puzzle pieces fit together, and at some point she, like a boy, will be successful and, as a result, proud of herself.

The more creatively active we are, the more worthy we feel. That's why it's so important not to give children too many fully assembled playthings; it's better for them to make things themselves and experiment with them. The Swedish author Astrid Lindgren wrote a very beautiful story about this, called 'The

Princess who did not want to play', in which a pampered princess becomes terribly bored in her castle. Surrounded by her toys, she doesn't know how to play. When Maja, a child who knows how to play and has a lively imagination, arrives with a simple wooden doll, she initiates a wonderful playtime for both of them.

These days, some preschools have toy-free days. Preschool teachers know that children come up with good play ideas by themselves, and can play extremely well with furniture, paper, glue and natural materials like sand, water, wood and stones. Children who are able to occupy themselves with very little, and who learn that they can intervene in events through their own actions, become self-confident, emotionally strong adults who are less likely to be defenceless victims of external circumstances.

Dealing with fear

Every child feels fear sometimes. But whereas men are expected to not show their fears, women – and especially girls – are allowed to. This is probably why they are more likely to admit to being afraid than boys and men are.

Jerome Kagan, Professor of Psychology at Harvard University, examined boys' and girls' fears in a longitudinal study – that is, a study of one group of children over some years – and found that even as toddlers, girls are more fearful than boys.[2] While both genders reacted, as babies, in the same way to new, unknown stimuli such as a strong odour or a brightly coloured hanging mobile – they were curious, but not afraid – there were already sharply defined differences in response at the age of fourteen months. The more fearful children – mainly girls – had an increased heart rate, larger quantities of stress hormones in their blood, their faces were more tense and their pupils were enlarged. These signs indicate activity in the amygdala, an almond-shaped nucleus in our brain's limbic system, which registers and sets off fear. Because androgens (male hormones) have a calming effect on the nerve cells in the amygdala, boys show less fear.

But Kagan also believes that, biological differences notwithstanding, excessive fear in girls is connected to overprotective caring they might receive from parents and minders. If you allow children to have quite normal experiences, which include accidents like falling over or slipping, they learn to deal with such mishaps as a matter of course – regardless of whether they're boys or girls.

It has been observed that parents often encourage their little girls to give up, because they – the parents – regard certain things as too dangerous, or unsuitable, for girls. For example, many boys are told to protect themselves against anyone who is aggressive towards them, but girls are told to accept things and to suppress aggressiveness.

Accepting feelings

Anger is a feeling everyone knows, and it has an important function: it helps us take responsibility for ourselves and tackle tasks – in short, it gives us courage. People who suppress anger are living unhealthily. Sooner or later, suppressed anger will emerge as a stomach ache, a headache, or as fear. Our own 'bad feelings', which we are not supposed to have, unconsciously return to us – often as 'monsters' or 'the big, bad wolf'.

Fear, too – and this cannot be emphasised enough – is, like every other feeling, meaningful and useful. Our fear warns us to watch out for ourselves, to come to terms with the reality of a risky situation. Fear helps us prepare for difficult or unknown circumstances. Instead of allowing ourselves to be overwhelmed by fear and paralysed into helplessness, we can use it. Fear is energy that can help us solve a problem or deal with a task.

How to manage a new and scary situation

Take a visit to the dentist, for example. It is completely normal to be frightened of something new. Say to your daughter, 'I understand that you're afraid. Whenever we do, or are about to try, something new, we're afraid. That's exactly why you should try it – it's only by doing this that you can get over your fear.' Explain to her that fear helps us get ready for a new situation: 'I'm afraid, but I'm going to do it anyway.' That's a very important sentence, because it reminds us of our own strength. Talk about what will happen at the dentist's. Once the dentist visit is successfully completed, your child will feel stronger. 'It's over – I managed it. In spite of my fear. I've overcome my fear!' That's an incredible feeling!

The more often your child has this positive experience, the better she will handle her own fear. Remind your daughter that at first she didn't want to ride a bicycle, but then she learned how to do it; that she was frightened of water, but now likes swimming; that she once didn't want to go to school, but now loves it.

How to reduce fear

As well as dealing with specific situations, as outlined in the box above, there are a few other things you can do that are in themselves good for your daughter, and that, as a side effect, will help her deal with fear:

- Increase your daughter's physical skills. By exploring our physical strengths, we also learn to control our body, and that gives us increased physical confidence, which in itself reduces fear (see pages 141–2). This skill-building can start with some of the simple games which fathers, in particular, tend to play with their daughters – for example, they lift them high up and let them 'fly' – and continues with playful scuffles and sports like horse riding. Gymnastics is great for physical skills, and you can learn to do simple exercises with your child. Be careful here not to make comparisons between your children! See what your child enjoys and follow that, encouraging her to do physical exercise that extends her skills.

- Singing is also a good way to counter fear – we don't say 'Whistle when you're in the dark' for nothing! If you often sing with your daughter for no particular reason, she'll build up a repertoire of songs that may be useful to her in many situations. There are also CDs and cassettes to help children cope with fear. Don't leave your daughter alone to play these

– sing them aloud together. Every time your daughter feels a sense of achievement, she is increasing her confidence and reducing her fear.

- Relaxation exercises are also a proven means of coping with fear. A person who knows how to make herself relax can handle fear-inducing situations more confidently. Include some fantasy journeys and relaxation exercises in your 'goodnight' storytelling. This will give your daughter a real treasure for her journey through life. You'll find ideas for this in any library, as there are many picture books that tell stories of children who have mastered their fears.

Reducing fear with a fantasy journey

Regardless of religious beliefs, many children find the idea of a guardian angel – a kind and gentle celestial being who has come down to Earth and always watches over them – very comforting. This can be used to help reduce fear in your daughter, especially as she is drifting off to sleep at night.

Journey to your guardian angel

Make yourself quite comfortable ... and feel how your breath is rising and falling, all by itself ... feel your feet ... your legs ... your hips ... and your stomach ... Let your stomach go soft and feel how it moves with your breath ... Feel your back ... your chest ... your shoulders ... And then imagine that you can send your breath down through both of your arms when you exhale, so that it exits through your fingertips (longer pause) ... Now feel your neck, your head ... your chin ... your upper and lower jaw are not touching ... your tongue is lying gently on the roof of your mouth ... your cheeks are soft and relaxed ... And now imagine that the next breath you draw goes right through your body, so that it leaves through your toes ... and with your next exhaled breath, imagine that the breath sprays out of the top of your head like a whale's ... And now imagine that your breath has got a colour that is doing you good ... so that sooner or later you are being wrapped up in a sphere of coloured light ... And you're lying there safe and sound ... Now you can go on a journey in your sphere ... to the stars or to the moon ... and sooner or later you'll see your guardian angel ... Perhaps you meet her or just guess where she is ... but you feel this sensation of safety and cosiness ... Perhaps your guardian angel is sending you a comforting message right now ... a word ... or a beautiful picture ... and in the certainty that you can go on a trip to your guardian angel at any time, you are now floating in your sphere back to Earth ... back to this room ... And you are stretching yourself now ... and you're here again now, refreshed and awake.

Parents' fears

Parents are always afraid for their children. No wonder – they know the dangers children are faced with these days. This fear is necessary, to a certain degree, because it warns us to take our parental duties seriously and protect our child from danger. Children have to be strapped into cars, cleaning agents must be locked away from them, hot water and hot drinks should not be left within reach of unattended toddlers, swimming pools must be fenced … and lots more. Responsible parents know all this, but still, most children have accidents at home.

It's important for parents to understand that children may be even more likely to have accidents if you constantly protect them from experience. For example, a child must learn how to fall over in order to learn how to stop herself falling over. I cannot stress this enough – falling over is an important and necessary childhood experience!

The brave and the not-so-brave

You will have already noticed that some children are 'cautious' and others are 'daredevils', and that this applies to girls as well as boys. Cautious children should be encouraged and prompted to test themselves. 'Daredevils' should be permitted to have the experiences they need – and desire! – but in a protected setting.

If your daughter is a daring 'rascal', support her. Foster her natural talent, even if it doesn't fit into the current 'girl' scheme of things or doesn't match your own ideas about girls. The parent who cultivates the strengths of her child has an easier time of it than the parent who keeps trying to eliminate weaknesses. Go along with the sheer exhilaration of her energy! Everything your child is allowed to do, she will learn how to do – and everything she has learned makes her proud. This pride in her own skills is the basis of stable and strong self-esteem, and that is the best guarantee that your daughter will become neither a culprit nor a victim. As a rule, both culprits and victims have weak self-esteem. I shall return to this subject later.

Parents protect their child best when they show her everything that can happen in everyday life. Show your daughter how a door closes and opens, for example, and which places around doors little fingers can get stuck in. Show her how to open and close drawers. Demonstrate (carefully!) to your child that a lit match and the teapot are hot, that a knife has a sharp edge, and that it's better to slide off a couch using your legs than your head. You are actually protecting your children if you allow them to climb trees and roll down hillsides, to balance, to splash about and to walk backwards. Children learn by experience – and being able to gather experience in a protected setting is their best protection against accidents.

Fears that are specific to girls

There are some fears that are specific to girls, and no-one can quite detach themselves from them. From time to time these fears are manifested publicly – when a girl is assaulted, raped and murdered, or when a girl simply disappears. What men can do to women – and in some cases what fathers have done to their daughters – haunts all parents of girls.

How should you feel about all this, and how should you respond to your feelings? First of all, stand by your fear. It doesn't help to suppress it.

On the contrary, take a good long look at it. What feeds it? Have you had experiences with (sexual) violence yourself? If you have, you should try to come to terms with your experiences with a therapist, so that you don't unconsciously transfer your fears to your daughter. This is the only way a disastrous cycle can be broken.

If you have had no personal experience of violence, your fears may be based on newspaper accounts, books and television. When a girl is murdered somewhere, it's news. And yet girls die daily – in accidents or from illness – and those deaths are not considered newsworthy. So we know that reality is represented in a distorted way by the media. This is likely to mean that your fear has been generated, to a large degree, by the media. Perhaps it will help if you remind yourself of a simple way in which many of us show that the media's portrayal of life is not balanced, and does not control our behaviour: most of us drive a car whenever we need to, without thinking twice about it, although we know that the chance of having a car accident is far greater than the risk of falling victim to an act of violence.

Take nothing for granted

The possibility of losing your child is always present. That should make you see that every day you spend with your child is a good day. There is no better protection than trust and faith! And each smile together counts. If you knew your child would die tomorrow, would you behave differently today?

German bishop and social commentator Dr Margot Kässmann has commented on this issue: 'On the one hand, it is overtaxing children to burden them now with the permanent worry of a "paedophile", which, on the other hand, ignores the fact that assault and rape offenders are often relatives and friends. Our fears and precautions are steered in the wrong direction. It is always stressed that self-confidence is the best way of guarding against assault. That is why it's important to strengthen it, rather than spread fear, which diminishes you.'[3]

The problem of 'learned helplessness'

Through psychological tests, it has been established that individual children cope in different ways with difficulties, and that those differences are independent of gender. In one test, with children who were at the same intelligence and educational level, some reacted to difficult tasks with increased effort, while others became confused and finally could not even deal with the tasks any more, even when the tasks were ones they'd managed with ease earlier.

Where does this difference come from? The children who persisted with the tasks gave themselves a positive pep-talk; they were not put off by their mistakes, and predicted a successful outcome for themselves. While the other children resigned themselves to failure and said, 'I can't do this!', these ones were saying, 'I'll try again. Sooner or later, it'll work out!' During this test, more girls than boys gave up, although these girls were of above-average intelligence in relation to the group.

Another study points in the same direction.[4] Girls and boys were asked why they achieved a good result in a particular test. While most boys put their good performance down to their own intelligence and industry, many girls said they did well because the tasks were quite easy; that is, they put their good performance down to favourable external circumstances rather than to their own strengths and abilities. The reverse is also true: boys commonly attribute failure to external sources, while girls tend to attribute it to themselves.

These results contain important warnings for parents. If your daughter makes mistakes, encourage her to use what she learns from the failure: 'That didn't work, so what does that tell us?' and then, 'I'm sure you can do it – there must be another way.'

Thinking can make it so

Learned helplessness is based on the underlying conviction that there is no connection between your own actions and the outcome or result. Put simply, it is a belief that 'It doesn't matter what I do – it won't work anyway!' Does this sentence have a familiar ring to it? If you watch a toddler playing, you'll see her pleasure in experimenting. She's having fun finding the right opening for a shape, making noise with pot lids, baking mud pies or climbing a ladder.

When parents interrupt this natural urge to discover with comments like, 'Leave it alone – you won't be able to do it!', or 'No, that's too hard!', the child will become more and more dejected. Soon she may start thinking, 'I won't be able to do this, however hard I try!'

Even adults have this reaction. Everyone interprets reality in their own way. The joke about the horse dung puts this well. Two people get horse dung for their birthday. One of them is horrified and thinks, 'This sort of shit always happens to me'; the other thinks, 'Hurray, I got a horse. But it's run away – I have to find it!'

People who don't give up easily and do believe in themselves assume that everything changes constantly: if you can't manage something today, you might be successful tomorrow. Moreover, they look at problems as challenges, things to be dealt with. And if they fail, they don't automatically blame themselves: they do some lateral thinking and look for ways around the problem, or strategies that might lead to a good outcome.

Errors are necessary, and it is important not to judge them negatively. They should be seen as a spur to finding creative solutions.

Parents, therefore, need to work out how they can encourage their daughter and strengthen her belief in herself and her capabilities. Use positive statements like, 'You'll get it!' and, 'You can do it!' These statements foster persistence and reinforce your daughter's trust in her own competence. They will help save her from the humiliating, resigned stance of a victim.

Unfortunately, in our society it is very common to criticise our children and to compare them with other children. This also takes us in the wrong direction. Comparisons don't motivate; they discourage. Remember, every child is unique and has her own set of abilities, knowledge and experiences.

Fantasy journeys for adventurous girls (from the age of three)

The following fantasy journeys are only samples. You can create simple adventures yourself for your daughter, including your favourite kinds of characters. During this, your daughter can lie down or sit peacefully, with eyes open or closed.

An animal in the forest

Make yourself quite comfortable … Do you feel the earth underneath you? … It is carrying you … And now imagine that you're in a beautiful forest … Look around you … perhaps you can hear particular sounds? … Or smell something? … Or feel? … All at once, you discover a small, cute animal … Let yourself be surprised by what kind of animal it is … Perhaps you wish to stroke it … Perhaps you want to tell it something … Or does the animal tell you something? … Now it's time to say goodbye to your animal … In your imagination, you can keep on meeting it … Now move your hands and feet and come back into the room, refreshed and awake.

Mountain climbing

Imagine we're climbing a very high mountain … It is stony, but you're very careful where you place your feet … You know how to do it … We are climbing higher and higher … Above us is the sun … It warms you … Now we're right up on the peak, gazing down into the valley … See how small the houses look from up here? And the cars? And the people? … When we have taken everything in, we climb back down … We are proud … And so we come back into the room, move our hands and feet and are refreshed and awake.

Dolphins

Today we're going to the beach ... It's a warm day, and we're looking out to sea ... There, we see a dolphin spring out of the water! ... And another one! ... Now we feel like swimming ... We run into the clear water ... Whoosh, how we splash! ... We are swimming over to the dolphins ... And playing with them ... And then we say goodbye to them and swim back to shore ... We know we'll meet again another time ... And then we return from the beach to this room, move our hands and feet and are refreshed and awake.

Overcoming obstacles (from the age of five)

Today you are going to ride on your favourite horse ... Let yourself be surprised at what colour he is and what he looks like ... He likes you ... You can feel that ... And now you can mount ... You are riding the horse ... To a place you like very much ... Have a look around there ... Feel the special power of this place ... Feel his strength, this pleasure ... You both ride along your favourite path ... Now there's an obstacle in the way, but you know you'll overcome it ... Done! ... Yes, you're a great team ... And now ... Another obstacle! ... You take it on ... You keep riding for a while ... Until you're both here again ... Say goodbye to your horse ... Until the next ride ... And then move your hands and feet and come back into the room, refreshed and awake.

The flying carpet

Just imagine a lovely, colourful carpet ... It is cosily soft and you like lying on it … And you know this carpet can fly … Carefully, it takes off … It sails with you out of the window … Down there, your friend is walking along … You wave to her … It ascends higher and higher … And you know how to steer the carpet … You know how to let it go higher and make it go lower … And then you have a look at what you've wanted to see for a long time … Perhaps it's the zoo … Or another city … The ocean … Or something quite different … And when you've had enough of your journey, you fly back home … Then the carpet comes to rest in your room … And you return and move your hands and feet, refreshed and awake.

Girls and pets – a great combination

Many girls – and boys, for that matter – adore having a pet, and many others would love to have one. Children should become familiar with animals and learn to look after them. Of course I'm not trying to talk you into getting a pet if you don't want one – in such a case, the animal would probably be neglected. I can assure you, though, that animals can enrich your life tremendously, if you are prepared to take them on.

If your daughter wants a pet, just remember that the youngest age she can look after it on her own is around eight. If you give her a pet when she's younger than that, you will have to constantly help her and remind her again and again of her tasks.

Pets at school

If you decide against having a pet, perhaps you could ask your daughter's school to keep some. This is already happening in many schools, so it's a very reasonable request. During recess at one school I know of, the girls usually race off to their rabbits, guinea pigs and even horses – while the boys play football. The positive side effect of this is that there is significantly less-than-average aggression and violence in the school!

After school, there are always several parents in the schoolyard spending time with their children caring for the pets. The school where my brother teaches keeps plants, mice, fish and more – they are looked after by a team of students, and there are more girls on the team than boys.

People who learn to be responsible for an animal are well positioned to look after a child carefully later. This is because by observing animals closely, which you do when you look after them, you gain sensitivity. Animals also give you a lot back: they don't reject you – the way people sometimes do – and they love you unconditionally. This experience can be very important and rewarding for children.

Girls and horses – an intimate relationship

During infants and primary school years, both boys and girls are equally drawn to horses and other animals, but a downright mania for horses begins for many girls during pre-puberty. Toy manufacturers have created many variations on horses, and these will initially satisfy many girls. These toys allow them to connect with horses on a symbolic level, and in their horse games they can express everything that moves, worries or preoccupies them. Between the ages of six and thirteen, my daughter and a girlfriend often played for ten hours and longer with toy horses – the games were only broken by meals. In other similarly intense games, she would slip into the horse's role herself.

In the long term, however, it's all about real horses. Men may dominate the top-level equestrian events, but in normal stables and horse-riding clubs there are more girls and women than boys and men. Why do horses have such a great attraction for girls?

In countless myths and stories handed down through history, the horse has been man's companion. Apart from the dog, there has been no animal that has served man with such versatility, and that remains true to this day. No-one would have expected that after the 1950s, when horses disappeared from agriculture, horses would still be kept and bred in such large numbers. The horse is an archetypal symbol, an animal with whom mankind can communicate in a special way. Horse-riding requires mental communion, intimate contact and trust.

In myths, there are several special kinds of horses: there are winged horses that conquer time and space and maintain contact with the gods. There are unicorns, which are especially beautiful and magnificent. There are centaurs, with a horse's body and a human's head and chest – which could be interpreted as a symbiosis of the instinctive animal with the detached rational human.

What horses can mean to girls

German psychiatrist and author Dörte Stolle writes, 'As a partner in the relationship, the horse is undemanding and free of cares. Girls test out questions like, "What suits me? What do I want to be?" with the horse. And the horse, their horse, conveys that compromises are also feasible without loss of dignity, and adaptability does not mean submission. Qualities that at first look like opposites – greatness, strength and speed versus submission and obedience – can be combined in this powerful companion, which encourages the young rider to try it out herself.'[5]

A girl thus learns that modes of behaviour like empathy and gentleness, in combination with their opposites – such as assertiveness and exercising power – can work for the horse, for herself on horseback, and for herself in everyday life. Horses strengthen girls' willpower and assertiveness because the girls must always assert themselves with the horse, while also taking responsibility for the horse and keeping to rules. In addition, working with horses improves body perception, coordination and balance.

'The horse seems well suited to convey to girls, in many ways, the pulse that they need for a transition into adult life,' adds Stolle. 'When riding and grooming this symbolic animal, they feel protection and security, but also autonomy and power.'

Perhaps horses are particularly well suited to symbolising and carrying the desires and anxieties of girls. Certainly, girls seem to allow themselves to be accompanied, comforted, carried off (in both senses) and encouraged by horses. For myriad reasons, girls love horses, and it does them good to associate with them. A girl who learns how to get on with a horse will gain a lot of self-confidence, because a horse is always stronger than a human being, but permits itself to be guided and directed.

Learning to ride

Girls as young as five can start at dressage schools. In time, they will gain such assurance that riding and guiding a horse will become easy. By the way, this group sport is also cheaper than riding with a club. Girls are also welcomed as helpers in many stables.

For children with a disability, there are therapeutic riding schools, and they are often very helpful. Even children who are severely handicapped loosen up on a warm horse, and they find a great deal of pleasure in the movement and in being with the horse. Horse-riding is also beneficial for children with behavioural disturbances and retardation – working with horses seems to help them learn how to keep to rules and act responsibly.

Owning a horse

If you live in the country, perhaps you already have a horse, or have ready access to one. Keeping a horse or a pony may not be too expensive if you can keep it with other horses in a communal stable. As girls usually become more interested in boys than horses after puberty, you may be able to find a pony or horse being sold cheaply. Bear in mind that there will also be costs for hoof care, vet visits and feed. In many cases, it may be more suitable to share your ownership of a horse.

In short, if you can arrange for your daughter to have an active interest in horses, you'll be doing her a lot of good.

In a nutshell

- Self-esteem is the cornerstone of your daughter's emotional development, and it also helps reduce fears.
- A girl's self-esteem is likely to be higher when she has a good relationship with her dad.
- So-called 'negative' emotions like fear and anger are perfectly normal, and should not be suppressed.
- We all want to protect our girls from harm, but if they are to learn important 'survival' skills, we must not be overprotective.
- Beware the trap of 'learned helplessness' – encourage self-belief and a 'can-do' attitude in your daughter.
- Pets can play an important role in your daughter's emotional development and her sense of responsibility.

Singing for her supper

When my daughter, Tessa, was five, our family went for dinner at a bar that permitted children in certain areas. One of these areas was where a karaoke competition was going on. A stream of men and women, mostly pretty drunk, got up and sang their favourite shower tune, took the scattered applause, and resumed drinking. Then Tessa decided she wanted a go. She's always been a great music lover, and her favourite group at the time was the Spice Girls. And her favourite Spice Girls song was 'Stop'. So I got the attention of the karaoke organiser, and a few songs later it was

Tessa's turn. I knew she was very nervous, but she strode up to the stage with great determination, took the (huge-looking) microphone in her little hand, and burst into her rendition of 'Stop' in perfect time with the backing track. She forgot the words at only one place in the song, which was great, and through her entire performance she did not move an inch. She stood completely rigid, looking mostly at the opposite wall and occasionally at the familiar faces in the crowd. When she finished, the room shook with applause.

I've never got up to sing karaoke in my life, and don't expect I'll start now. I was so proud of Tessa and her courage. She has never shied away from a challenge and has always been keen to try something new. May that never change!

Sean

Taking it all in

Our daughter is like a sponge. The amount she has learned in the past few months since starting school is just amazing. Just last night I said to my husband in code, 'Do you want to go and S.E.E S.H.R.E.K. on W.E.D.N.E.S.D.A.Y.?'

My daughter turned around knowingly and said, 'Yes, I want to see Shrek on Wednesday.'

I turned to my husband and said, 'She's too C.L.E.V.E.R.'

And she announces, 'I'm clever, aren't I?'

Did she guess all this or not? I'm not quite sure, but she certainly is one smart cookie.

The other amazing thing is her fascination with drawing, writing and making things – anything. As soon as she is out of bed in the morning till the time she goes to bed at night, she is constantly doing something, asking questions about how to do it or how to spell something so that she can do a card or letter. I hope that this enthusiasm for creating and learning doesn't fade in a few years because she is certainly blossoming as a result, and I would hate to see it end.

Debbie

FIVE

HOW SOCIETY CONDITIONS GIRLS

You probably have a good idea about whether the first day of (pre)school is going to be easy or difficult for your daughter as she enters society. Many children approach this situation with curiosity rather than anxiety, but others find it difficult and need time to adjust. And it's the same for mothers and fathers: many will find it quite easy to see their daughters move into the world, while for others, merely thinking about it makes their heart heavy.

When your daughter begins her life at an educational institution – whether it is a preschool, a childcare centre or a primary school – the ideal introduction is for her to get used to both the place and the teacher with a parent present. Then, one day, she will stay there willingly by herself. The time children spend in such institutions, and what happens to them there, helps mould them. Perhaps your daughter will be in a group for the first time, or with boys for the first time. As well as many wonderful experiences, she'll also have to suffer disappointments and overcome conflicts.

For many years now, teachers and parents have been trying to overcome gender stereotyping in schools. Why this is needed is clear from the following example. Five-year-old Eva is playing with a ball. Then Lucas, who is the same age, comes over and takes it from her. Eva starts to cry and complains to the teacher, who just answers, 'Don't tell tales all the time!'

In this case, the teacher has backed the boy's behaviour and not gone to the root of the conflict. The girl has been accused and humiliated. Another teacher could react by saying, 'Typical boy! It's just impossible the way they carry on!' And she'd punish Lucas.

Neither of these approaches would help Eva or Lucas. Both responses just reinforce stereotypical gender roles. A more thoughtful teacher might challenge Eva to defend herself – and support her when she tries to get the ball back. This teacher would not dismiss Lucas either; she would discuss with him ways he could go about getting the ball that don't involve just snatching it.

Be active in your daughter's school and help to ensure that girls and boys are not expected to fill the old, handed-down roles

Gender stereotypes and what to do with them

Parents can help to ensure that girls and boys are treated fairly and without old-fashioned gender role expectations in the preschool – and, for that matter, the primary school – that their daughter attends. On parent–teacher evenings, mothers, fathers and teachers can work together to help make the school a prejudice-free zone. All these adults have the opportunity to embed new conduct and new areas of experience into the children's routine.

The use of role-plays in school is particularly useful because it can prompt boys and girls to take on roles that are opposite to their natural ones. Don't do this with children younger than five years old, though: younger children have just discovered their gender identity, and they need – with partly exaggerated behaviour – to give it a road-test before they can safely experiment with it.

I myself have had good experiences with acting out picture books and fairytales with children. When the role-playing is about fun, rather than being part of an ambitious, stress-filled formal production, everyone can enjoy and learn from it.

When you are choosing a school for your daughter – if a choice is available – read the school's statement of educational goals, and look for what it says about gender roles. If you're not happy with the statement, talk to the staff and clarify the school's position – and try to change it if you feel it is inappropriate. This is important because the statement is what you will need to refer to if you ever need to discuss incidents involving your daughter.

For individual activities, there are times when it may be sensible to separate boys and girls and work in single-gender groups – but not because girls are 'better' at one thing and boys are 'better' at another. When boys are doing woodwork without any girls, for example, they have to comfort each other if one of them hurts himself, because there is no girl nearby to take on the role of comforter. In the girls' group, some may be able to demonstrate their manual dexterity, and so serve as an example for other girls. In this way, both girls and boys are able to break out of the confines of gender stereotypes.

Expressing anger

As we know, girls often suppress their anger and aggression; they bottle it up. Some girls direct these feelings towards themselves, which then leads them to devalue themselves and perhaps not express themselves as freely as they usually do. In extreme cases, some even kill themselves. The general rule holds true for all girls (and indeed for boys as well): not dealing with anger and aggression is unhealthy. It leads to poor self-esteem, and the results of this run through all aspects of a person's life. So while playground problems between girls and boys may seem like tiny things, how teachers deal with them is very important.

> 'If girls are already supported in preschool to recognise and take their anger seriously,' and are given the opportunity, for example, to test their strength, they will learn that responsibility for others and self-assertion go hand in hand, just as harmony and conflicts do.'
>
> **– Dörte Stolle**

How Girls Relate

Many parents will have seen their one-year-old daughter get a toy truck from Santa and not show a scrap of interest in it – not even when her dad tried to make the gift more appealing to her. For most girls, boys' toys are uninteresting – even my three sons' colourful Lego blocks left my daughter cold. She wanted dolls and horses!

Linguist Deborah Tannen and many other female scientists have proved that even very little girls behave differently from little boys.[2] Social contacts are very important to girls, and even at the age of three, many have a 'best friend' – a relatively mature concept. Whether or not they 'belong' means a great deal to girls. If you tell a story about feelings to three-year-old girls, they display a clearly defined, social way of thinking insofar as they 'understand' what feelings are and how they can affect the person experiencing them as well as others around him or her. When playing in a group, girls try to negotiate compromises and be considerate, so as not to upset their girlfriends. Boys at this age, in contrast, often fight each other in order to establish a pecking order.

Deborah Tannen asked pairs of best friends of preschool age – of both sexes – to take two chairs into an empty room and occupy themselves. The little girls immediately sat down close to each other and started talking, maintaining eye contact. The boys experimented with putting the chairs in different places; they had very brief verbal interchanges, and hardly looked at each other.

As soon as girls know that they'll become women, they become preoccupied with having children, babies and nursing. I can still remember very well how my sons, at about two years of age, held their dolls to imaginary breasts. After a little while, when they realised they would never have children, the dolls flew into a corner and were not brought out again.

Toys for little girls

What I have listed below are simple things that are available in almost every household.

Toys for the first six months:
(these should all be large enough not to fit in the mouth, to avoid choking hazards)

- Non-toxic materials such as lids, fabrics, cloths, wooden objects
- Items of various shapes, such as rings, cubes and cups
- Simple chiming toys such as musical clocks or balls
- Sieves, funnels, water.

Toys for the seventh to the twelfth month:

- Natural foodstuffs such as carrots, bananas, apples
- Balls
- Various coverings and fabrics (for crawling on) such as cotton, wool, etc.
- Containers with screw-top lids (large enough not to fit into the mouth).

Toys for one year onwards:

- Carts for pushing and pulling
- Crawl tubes
- Sheets for building caves/cubbies
- Balls and balloons
- Chimes
- Simple drum sets
- Wooden building blocks.

Toys for the second year onwards:

- Accessories for role-playing games – caps, bags, wallets, flat surfaces to use as shop counters
- Dolls, stuffed animals
- Wax crayons, large sheets of paper
- Hand puppets
- Simple puzzles.

Toys for the third year onwards:

- Accessories for play scenarios such as puppet theatres, farmyards, castles
- Scissors
- Paintbox, glue
- Toolbox, workbench
- Doll's stove
- Doctor's bag.

I would like to stress, though, that there are always exceptions to these 'rules'. Not all girls are interested in dolls. Girls who want to play with building blocks, cars and cranes should be allowed to. It is not a good idea to try to influence your daughter and direct her attention towards a particular toy. On the contrary, support your daughter in her interests. Give her various stimuli. Follow her joy – that is her best motivation.

What should we do about Barbie?

We should pursue this question, which I have borrowed from Nicky Marone. She writes, 'Barbie is more than just a doll. She's the icon of modern femininity, a sacred image of men's fantasy run wild, and [she] undermines many young girls' self-confidence.'[3]

Barbie has been around – and adored – for 40 years, and millions of Barbies have been sold, so the chances are good that some day you too will be a parent of a daughter with a Barbie doll. It may not even be your daughter's doll.

Barbie looks exactly like a marketing strategist's idea of the average man's dream woman: a slender, long-legged young woman with long blonde hair and a full bust.

So what are you going to do about Barbie? For the time being, you should turn your attention back to yourself. Did you have a Barbie doll as a child? How did you go with it? Did you want to look like Barbie? Do you want to look like Barbie now?

Nicky Marone writes, 'Part of the problem lies in our own contradictory view of beauty. Most of us, given the possibility, would like to look like Claudia Schiffer or Cindy Crawford. So it's not about not wanting to look like Barbie. We're just resisting the pressure of having to look as beautiful.'[4] Examine your own beauty ideal before you decide whether or not to buy your daughter a Barbie doll. The pressure on women to look good is so great that most women bow to this dictate – and of course we pass this pressure to conform on to our daughters.

Shake up the clichés

In the end, either buying or not buying Barbie is okay. If you refuse to get a Barbie for your daughter, explain why. If you buy her one, it's not the end of the world. Either way, explain to her your own position on Barbie, and what feelings this doll triggers in you. Make it clear to her why latter-day Barbies have tilted feet, ready-made for high heels – and tell her all the things you cannot do in high heels. The problem, though, is that your daughter will take some convincing, because what really makes Barbie so attractive is that she is a grown woman, not a little girl like the other dolls.

Little girls are on the lookout for adult women, and they identify with them. What you can do to make Barbie a positive rather than a negative presence is to make her an expedition leader, a pilot or a scientist during play sessions with your daughter. In this way, at least you can have a little influence on your daughter's expectations. And you may even be able to rattle current clichés a little. What Nicky Marone says to Barbie's answering service may give you some ideas: 'Hello Barbie, this is Melissa. I have a few questions about the white-water rafting trip through the gorge that you're running this summer. What sort of equipment do I need? Do I need my own helmet and life jacket? What else?', or 'Hello Barbie, don't you remember me? I'm Dr Carol McIntyre, Professor of Environmental Science at Stanford University. Recently, I learned from a female colleague that you have just discovered a new type of solar cell ...'[5]

What do you do with Barbie? Make your own decision. I didn't buy my daughter a Barbie, but her Grandma did. If she hadn't, Barbie would have moved in with us via pocket money anyway. I explained to my daughter why I don't like Barbie. In spite of this, she loved playing with Barbie. Then one day, Barbie was out – but soon my daughter had high-heeled shoes of her own. The truth is, of course, that not everything is under your control. And that's good. But you should always be allowed to give your opinion – and make sure you give it!

As an aside, I'd like to tell you a joke a friend told me. She has three daughters of her own – one of them, Lisa, told her the joke. A woman goes into a shop to buy a Barbie doll. The saleswoman shows her the various models: 'This is Horse riding Barbie, which costs £12. Here's Tennis Barbie, which is £13, and that's Wedding Barbie, for £15. And here we've got Divorced Barbie, which costs £50.'

'Why is this last one so expensive?' asks the woman, surprised.

'Because if you take that one, you also get Ken's villa, yacht and campervan.'

Why books are important

Today's children often get to know each other very early in life. As well as their own family, many of them know several other families quite well by the time they go to school – they meet other children and make friends in preschool, then play with them at home, and perhaps even have sleepovers.

But children can also get to know other children and other families through books. Television is not a substitute for books. Picture books can be browsed in silence – over and over, whenever the child feels like it. And even if the book is only text, with no pictures, the child will draw her own pictures to go with it, in her mind and also on paper. Both these are a creative achievement. Television is not – it is passive.

Your daughter's first picture books should be simple, with only one object per page. If you like doing such things, you can sew picture books out of cloth. Then your daughter can touch the very tactile pictures and use several of her senses at once. When you are choosing books for your daughter, choose ones that have females in them. But check them out first. Does the image of the girl/woman shown in these books match your ideas? Think back to your childhood. Who were the heroines of your childhood? Which books, films or plays did they come from?

Books influence us for our whole lives, so what you read to your daughter – and what your daughter reads herself, later on – is important. In addition to those mentioned above, you might like to consider the wonderful *Anne of Green Gables* series of books by L. M. Montgomery, and the *Little House on the Prairie* series by Laura Ingalls Wilder, both of which feature strong, assertive girls having lots of adventures. Go to the bookshop together; you will make some interesting discoveries.

My favourite childhood reading

As a girl, I read all the books by Erich Kästner, in which there are many strong girl characters. There is a great little girl with a fairly insensitive mother in *Annalouise and Anton*, and in *Lisa and Lottie* (which my sister and I both adored) the clever girls have lots of adventures.

I also loved Astrid Lindgren's books, and they are still not boring for me – even though I've probably read them aloud twenty times. In them, we meet Pippi Longstocking, who always does what she wants. She is an open-minded thinker full of humour and imagination. And naturally, she's strong – stronger than any man. Have you read *The Children of Bullerbü*? In this book Astrid Lindgren describes her own childhood. It's true that the girls wear dresses in this story, because trousers were not usual at the time, but they don't let themselves be fooled by the boys at all. They're actually superior to the boys in many things, and they know it. Though no-one is more inventive and funny than Lasse (who is based on the author's brother), the boys don't set the tone of all the games, and both girls and boys have to help their parents work. The children in Bullerbü have some shared games, but also others that only the girls play and that no boy would understand. And all the girls in Astrid Lindgren's books at some time or other climb onto the roof – I really love this metaphor. Being up on the roof is fantastic because you've got the right perspective!

Madita is another great character in an Astrid Lindgren book. Her father is a socially committed journalist, and she is very similar to him in many ways. She is a strong girl who knows what she wants to do and does it. She fights openly with Mia, another girl, but at the same time she is full of empathy and stands up for other people. Madita also invents wonderful games to play with her little sister. Would she have been able to do this if she sat in front of the television several hours a day? I don't think so.

Fairytales

In almost all fairytales, girls and women play a significant role. This alone is a reason for you to take them seriously.

Fairytales, like most things, should not be forced onto children. My daughter didn't like them very much when she was young, and only became interested in them as she grew older. Some children don't like them much, but others do: those children who feel drawn to them probably actually need them.

Did you have a favourite fairytale in your childhood? I had several, and although I've read and heard each of them about a hundred times all up, they are still a revelation to me every time. For me, these fairytales are a way of passing on age-old wisdom.

Take *Snow White*. In the original version, it's the mother – not the stepmother – who wants to kill her daughter. It's difficult for a woman to see her own beauty fade as her daughter becomes more and more beautiful. Envy poisons. Snow White's salvation takes place in the solitude of nature, behind the seven mountains. It occurs when she is with the dwarves, whom she serves. They cannot save her from death by poison, though; that is left to the Prince. He carries her along the bumpy, uneven path in the forest and the poisoned piece of apple in her mouth falls out. Now she is safe. There's a happy ending, as always – even when the story involves terrible tortures or awfully long journeys. Isn't this a comforting message?

In *King Lindwurm*, a German fairytale, a country is being threatened by a dragon. It's the shepherd's daughter who solves the problem, saving herself and her country – she gives the monster, a wingless dragon, his human shape back. She does this by following the advice of a wise old woman. It is not female cunning that does the trick; it is knowledge from a much deeper source.

In *Sleeping Beauty* the heroine, like Snow White, cannot escape her fate: only when it's the right time can the male saviour come and kiss her back to life. All the others who tried to reach her stay entangled in the thorns. (But why was the King so stubborn as to permit only twelve of the thirteen wise women to be invited to the feast?)

Fairytales teach us that nothing is impossible. They show us, figuratively, that difficulties always lead to salvation if you do not run away from finding a way through, from taking on the task. The person who keeps an open, good heart will gain access to the wisdom – generally in a natural setting such as in a forest, on the heath or in the mountains – that will lead them to their destination. The message is that by doing this, we can all win a kingdom.

Fairytales teach us that all problems can be solved as long as you accept the challenge, follow your own path and don't give up

Little girls and dressing up

My daughter had a strong interest in clothing from an early age. She was able to get dressed and undressed when she was very young, and she derived a lot of pleasure from changing her outfits, dressing up and trying on clothes. And as soon as she spied some nail polish somewhere, she wanted it. It was the same with jewellery. This behaviour surprised me, because she didn't get it from me – I don't attach much importance to any of those things – and she didn't watch television.

At the age of fourteen she appeared in front of me one day dressed in her black confirmation suit and high-heeled shoes. She was beaming, and said, 'I'm so looking forward to being able to wear stuff like this every day!'

'Why don't you do it now?' I asked, curiously.

'I don't need to yet,' she said, 'but when I have a professional job, I'll put on something like this every day.'

The many faces of beauty

There is every reason to believe that the female wish to be beautiful is socially conditioned, and it is a powerful force in the vast majority of societies. For centuries, women have busied themselves with the manufacture of textiles (woven, knitted, embroidered) and looked after all the tribe's clothing. The desire to have a beautifully furnished house and a beautiful body – the drive to make an artwork of yourself – is ancient.

Nearly every mother takes a lot of pleasure in fitting out her little daughter with fine clothes, beautiful shoes and jewellery.

And little boys are often not allowed to get dressed up – their parents may be afraid that if they do, they will be laughed at and called 'girls' (or 'gay' if they're older).

The media's depiction of women

The portrayal of women in magazines is a distorted image of reality, as we all know. Less beautiful women have only a marginal place there, if any. Women who do not conform to the ideal are filtered out, so we don't see them, even though such women are the majority. And for women who are professionally successful, the more beautiful they are, the more interesting they become – to the media, at least.

Mind you, it has also been proved that beautiful people don't always have it easy, because others have high expectations of them. From the start, they're expected to be smarter, more affectionate and more pleasant-natured. In addition, many beautiful women believe that they are regarded highly only because of their appearance, and that their achievements are not respected. That leads to unhappiness. These women never feel they are taken seriously. They feel their beauty is a mask they cannot remove – and this can lead to self-destruction, through alcohol, drugs or even suicide.

As a little girl, I too was fitted out in dresses and ribbons. In puberty I lost nearly all interest in these externals – and that has been the case ever since. Did I want to set myself apart from my older, prettier sister? Perhaps. In families with several girls, each girl takes on a separate role. When the role of 'the pretty one' is taken, the next daughter has to choose another role. She might play 'the intelligent one' or 'the nice one', or 'the rebel' (for more on the importance of birth order, see Chapter 8). Or perhaps I internalised my father's motto – that inner values counted the most. Or perhaps I just chose a different life's work.

Your daughter and her life's work

After having observed and studied children for 30 years, I believe each child has a life's work that she is trying to fulfil. You can start to see what your daughter's task is by observing her interests and what gives her pleasure, because pleasure comes from the heart; it cannot be artificially created by external circumstances. For example, I played intensively with dolls for years, and treated them as my children. For me, a life without studying children is unimaginable, even if I had not had any children myself.

In adulthood, many people accept society's and their family's norms and conditions and expectations. They then do things they really do not want to do because of these external pressures, and in this way they change themselves, and sometimes turn away from their life's work. People don't find happiness this way – true happiness comes when you find and fulfil your own personal life's work.

When they are small, your children will show you very clearly which way their tendencies lie – and this applies equally to girls and boys.

The word 'education' seems less and less useful to me. In my view, what you should be doing as parents is better described as 'development', in the literal sense – going along with your child as she discovers what her life's work is, helping her develop her abilities. This is what schools should be doing, too. In order to really find out what your child needs, just observe her attentively and offer her things. Do not force her in any direction.

In a nutshell

- Reflect on your own preconceptions about girls in our society.
- Give some thought to the toys, dolls, etc. that your daughter plays with, and show her there is life beyond Barbie.
- Girls continue to receive unrealistic and damaging messages about body image from the media.
- Teach your daughter to not be limited by social conditioning.
- Books, and especially fairytales, can be a wonderful source of empowering ideas for girls.
- Reading, unlike watching TV, spurs the imagination and creative life of a child.

Wishing upon a shooting star

Just the other evening I was getting out of the car with my 11-year-old daughter when she said, 'I want to show you the Southern Cross, Dad.'

'Great,' I replied. 'Let's check it out.'

We walked up the driveway and turned towards the southern sky, and at that very moment a star went shooting across the sky right in front of us. I've seen plenty of shooting stars in my time, but this was something special. It sped in a line parallel to the horizon, it shone for a long time, and it was very bright. It was so bright, in fact, that it seemed to be so much closer than all the other visible stars. Some death!

What was most special about it, though, was that it was the first shooting star that my daughter had ever seen.

'Wow! What a beauty,' I breathed, gazing up in wonder.

'Make a wish!' she cried as she closed her eyes and held her hands up, palms together as if in prayer. (We don't formally pray in our family, and nor does my daughter pray at school, so it was very interesting to see her make this gesture.)

Maybe I should have wished for something beyond the usual 'May everyone in the family have a happy and healthy life', but I didn't. Instead I watched her as she wished for something important. I wanted to ask her what, but I knew she wouldn't tell me (because then it won't come true) so I didn't bother. She wants to be a vet when she grows up – was it this she wished for? I don't know; probably not. But if she did, I thought at the time, I am thankful that we live in a world where such wishes can come true. She can be anything she wants to be, and that helps to make me a happy dad.

Sean

SIX

SCHOOLS AND LEARNING

In addition to the nurturing you give your daughter at home and the lessons she learns from you there, you must also be aware of the messages she receives from society at large. Let's now turn to the third significant source and focus of her experience: school.

The news isn't all good

In school, girls are often ahead of boys the same age in many areas. They adapt more easily to school, learn to read and write more quickly, and generally create fewer problems. That's what the statistics say. However, the figures hide quite a lot.

Those girls who don't learn to read and write as quickly as the majority of girls stand out, and run the risk of being excluded from the group. This is especially bad for girls because, as a rule, the group means a lot to them.

Girls learn differently from boys – but this has not yet been taken into account in many of our schools. Running single-sex classes for science and technical subjects could be helpful in maximising girls' opportunities in subjects traditionally considered the domain of boys.

More broadly, school education should take into consideration the personal experiences of all the students – that is, it should somehow include the life history and personal interests of each child.

Choosing a school

The first thing you can do to help your daughter at school is – if possible – to choose a school that has the best possible conditions for her, and where she is likely to get as much pleasure as possible from learning. Unfortunately, in some schools, children's self-esteem is not supported much; sometimes it is even trampled on. This is a very difficult issue to tackle – but it is your duty to confront the school about it. Some children are described as 'reserved', others are 'too lively'. But what do these tags mean? Isn't there room for all types of children?

How to tell if a school is girl-friendly[1]

1   Does the school have policies about Equal Opportunity or Gender Equity that are actually applied, and that effectively counter racism and homophobia and heterosexism?

2   Do students know what to do if they're being harassed and bullied? Is there a policy about this, too?

3   Are there teachers who girls can approach to discuss personal matters? (They may not necessarily all be women.)

4 If the school is co-ed, are there any single-sex classes for young women for particular subjects or times?

5 Are the subjects 'gender inclusive'? Do they cover what both men and women do and experience, or do they pretend that all scientific discoveries and all of history is really only about men? And that girls only want to learn to cook and boys want to fix cars?

6 What does the school do for girls with disabilities?

7 Does the school organise girls-only use of particular facilities and spaces, e.g. computers, basketball courts, sports equipment?

8 Are girls represented equally on student committees and in school leadership?

9 How does the school listen to young women? How do girls have their say in school decisions being made?

10 Does the school uniform allow trousers, shorts and sensible shoes for young women as well as young men?

11 How does the school encourage young pregnant women and young mothers to continue their education?

12 What practices are in place to allow girls to leave class when they are menstruating? Is there a sanitary pad disposal unit in every female toilet cubicle? Or do girls have to face up to an office or sick room?

If your daughter has bad reports or other problems at school, it is especially important that you support her and show her that you love her despite these difficulties. If necessary, speak to the teachers and arrange for temporary extra tuition. Also, support your daughter in her interests. And observe her carefully so that you and she both find out which tasks she is good at and which she needs help with.

Girls and maths and science

As a rule, girls do worse than boys in standardised maths tests. There are various theories about why this is so. Some people believe there is a hormonally-based difference between boys' and girls' brains; others believe that girls are treated differently from boys at home and school, and that is why they do worse.

In 1995 and 1996, The Third International Mathematics and Science Study was carried out. It assessed half a million pupils in the fourth, eighth and twelfth grades in 21 countries. In maths and the sciences, boys in all the countries except South Africa achieved higher results than girls,[2] and the older they were, the greater the difference was. Although the respective differences within the girls' group and within the boys' group were greater than the differences between the genders, the test results did seem to prove that boys do better than girls in these study areas.

If one examines the results more closely, however, as author Susan Gilbert did, it becomes clear that these differences only applied to white students. Moreover, she established that non-white girls did better than non-white boys in arithmetic and other strands of maths. Thus, the decisive factor seems to be that many (white) parents think girls are less talented at maths than boys. And more importantly, it seems that the girls think the same thing.

By the beginning of puberty, girls' interest in maths diminishes. This puts them at a disadvantage, because maths is the basis for many areas of study. But should girls really study maths? Does it pay off for us? Evidently not always, according to Susan Gilbert. For together with their dislike of mathematical subjects, she claims that some girls accept the prejudices of their contemporaries: 'Whoever is good at maths is unattractive to the boys,' some of them say. I don't believe things are so simple. When I asked my fifteen-year-old daughter about this, she smiled and said she thought most boys would prefer an intelligent girlfriend. But even in her class, the maths geniuses are all boys.

When they get good marks, girls are usually praised for their industry rather than their intelligence

Learned helplessness and parents' roles

Girls often just give in to difficulties, instead of viewing their mistakes as a challenge and something they can use as a basis for improvement.

In a study carried out at Michigan University in the US in the 1980s, thousands of children were tested to identify the roots of the gender difference in achievement in maths.[3] The study questioned parents and children. During most of the primary school years, parents assessed the mathematical skills of their sons and daughters as relatively equal; however, by the time their children were at the end of primary school, the parents believed there were distinct differences. The parents who thought maths was particularly difficult for girls in fact underestimated their daughters' performance. If a girl brooded over her maths exercises at home, parents would pity rather than encourage her. And when girls got good marks, they were praised less for their mathematical skill than for their hard work. The doubts about the mathematical skills of girls also came from the girls themselves, which is hardly surprising.

Encouraging persistence

It is clear that if you treat girls differently when it comes to maths, and expect less of them, they are likely to get poorer maths results. This is how self-fulfilling prophecies work. This means that it is important for you to encourage your daughter in all her schoolwork, and indeed in all other areas of endeavour. Girls can achieve good results in maths, just as boys can; the issue is what is expected of them, and thus what they expect of themselves. This observation echoes what we noted earlier about how parents react to girls when they make a mistake or fail at a task (see pages 67–9). You need to encourage persistence, because it shows that you believe your daughter can succeed in the task in the end, and this belief is what builds her self-esteem.

A learning difference

US psychologist David C. Geary investigated how girls and boys go about solving tasks, and discovered that boys see exercises pictorially, or as images, whereas girls respond better to material presented in spoken or written form.[4] He recommended that teachers and parents of boys represent verbally formulated tasks graphically, and was successful in this.

Styles of learning

My own opinion about maths is that it is quite often taught using limited materials that don't suit girls' preferred styles of learning, and that's why girls fail. A friend of mine once showed me the maths material used in Montessori schools. It is clear and simple – extremely appealing to the eye. After first explanations, children can work with it and discover a lot themselves. I am sure that if I had been taught with such materials, I would have understood maths.

However, girls are closing the gap in maths. The difference between boys' and girls' results is narrowing, and fewer people now believe the old ideas about girls being naturally inferior at maths. And time after time, we hear that girls have better school marks overall than boys.

However, there are still relatively few girls taking on technical or mathematical professions, even when they are doing well in these subjects at school. Why is this? Investigations have shown that many girls in coeducational schools feel devalued by the behaviour of their fellow students and teachers, and lose interest in academic success. Also, it seems that what girls perceive as society's expectations affect their choice of occupation. Girls still often feel they are expected to take up typically female occupations like primary school teaching, nursing and secretarial work. Many girls do not dare move into traditional men's domains such as engineering or technical professions.

Not all women want to reach the top

It is common knowledge that far fewer women than men reach top management positions. This happens even in traditional women's professions. When I recently discussed this with a social scientist, she said, 'Yes – but we women don't want those positions.' She herself (single and living alone) had declined several management positions because she didn't want the responsibility associated with them. Perhaps women have less desire for power. On the other hand, there are also many women struggling in what still feels like a man's world. Officially, women's promotion to the highest positions is possible, but the 'glass ceiling' seems to appear sooner or later, and they simply do not progress further – as a rule, without knowing why.

How to encourage your daughter

You have many opportunities to encourage your daughter so that she can be successful at school and choose an occupation that matches her likes and abilities. The following ideas might be helpful:

- Promote your daughter's spatial–visual imagination. Above all, spatial–visual skills develop through practice and experience with suitable toys. Let your daughter play with wooden building blocks and Lego. Sports activities also help improve her spatial–visual skills.
- Encourage your daughter not to give up, but to work at a solution. If she's having trouble with a particular task, try

saying things like, 'Maybe you haven't found the right method yet. Let's try it together', or 'If you don't manage it now, have a look at it later. Often you have a better idea when you come back to something after a break.'

And when it comes to maths:

- Have a look at the Montessori maths materials and use them if you think they would help your daughter be more confident and capable with maths.
- Encourage your daughter's mathematical talents by using mathematical questions in your normal conversation, 'There are five of us in the family. But Tom is at his friend's place, and Dad won't be home until late. How many places will we set at the table?' When you cook, recipes often have to be doubled or halved. Involve your daughter in this.
- As a father, involve your daughter in what are typically 'men's jobs'.
- If either parent (or both) has a job, encourage your daughter to take part in your professional work sometimes. This is not always possible, of course, but it may be more possible than you think if you apply a little creativity.
- Teach your daughter how to handle money and involve her in everyday money-counting tasks.
- Involve your daughter in any furnishing or home renovation tasks you are carrying out. There are calculations and measurements necessary here, as well.
- Give her a chance to have fun with maths and the sciences through experiment boxes, microscopes, telescopes, etc.

A visualisation exercise for positive learning

Make yourself comfortable and watch your breathing, how it comes and goes, all by itself … And then imagine that you are strolling through a lovely forest … You look around and notice a particularly beautiful tree … You want to wait here a bit … It is such a beautiful and peaceful place … All at once, you feel the presence of a kind fairy … She is a wise, loving, wonderful woman, who comes from a place where everything is possible … She wishes to teach you something, something that you want to learn … And now she is showing you what it is … And you've got all the time in the world, all the time you need, to watch closely or to listen to her … (long pause) … And now you say thank you and goodbye, in the certainty that you may return to this place at any time … Whenever the fairy wants to teach you something, you can return to this special tree … And when you've made sure that you remember everything along the path, you go back through the forest … And you come back here again, move your hands and feet, and you are completely returned, refreshed and awake.

In a nutshell

- Investigate how girl-friendly a school is before you send your daughter there.
- Girls' frequent underachievement in maths and science is mainly due to parental attitudes, inappropriate teaching materials and gender stereotyping in schools.
- You can make a big difference to how your daughter perceives her ability in different subjects.

Helping them achieve their (individual) dreams

I have two daughters who are 23 months apart in age. Each have similar talents in sport and artistic endeavours but, at the same time, very different abilities and goals. Elysia, my eldest, from the day she could walk at the age of 9 months, would climb everything in sight. This included a set of sturdy bookcases in the living room, which we kept empty so she could do this without any danger of knocking of things and hurting herself. Subsequently she never fell or tired of doing this favourite game.

As she grew up she showed some talent in athletics and sports generally, and always felt confident in her athletic ability. At the end of each school year she would be nominated for 'Sports Girl of the Year' and would be narrowly beaten in a very competitive field. Finally, in Year 10, she was nominated as Sports Girl for 2003 for the whole school, and she won. This was not only a very proud moment for her parents, who had enjoyed all of her sporting successes over the years, but also of course for Elysia herself, who had finally achieved a goal she had been seeking all of her years in junior high school. She has now given up a lot of her sporting interests, concentrating on weekend club soccer as the all-encompassing Senior years take over her life.

Ultimately, the enjoyment and confidence she has developed in her sporting activities will continue on when she is an adult and allow her to keep fit and healthy.

As for my other daughter, Allegra also enjoys soccer but has an interest in drama and now attends a Performing Arts High School. When she was in Year 4 she was able to express herself and be nurtured in the performing arts by the wonderful creative teachers at her school. Even at that age she was very clear in her mind that she wanted to go to a Performing Arts High School.

So, like all good parents, we helped her develop her talent. She never showed any fear or nervousness when performing and it was wonderful when she achieved her goal and was accepted into a Performing Arts High School. We thought this was wonderful – to be in such a creative environment. However, such an environment can be equally competitive and intimidating with a larger pool of talent. Allegra began to feel nervous about performing in front of her peers and started to miss out on some of the opportunities that the school provided. So what could we do but give her intensive drama classes to build her confidence back up, and give her experience in competitions to reduce her feeling of intimidation. Is it succeeding? Yes – bit by bit Allegra's confidence is returning, and hopefully will return to what it was in primary school. In the meantime she is still having what I think is a very exciting, creative and, interesting school life compared to what most of us experienced when we attended school in the Sixties.

Jeannette

SEVEN

BECOMING A YOUNG WOMAN

Puberty and the associated developmental steps are a great challenge for all children and their parents. While girls who are nine or ten are often strong and self-assured, by the time they are thirteen, fourteen or fifteen they are often confused, agitated and insecure.

This usually has less to do with parents than with the new role expectations they are facing.

Problems of adolescence

The problems of adolescence and early adulthood cannot always be solved by girls and their parents together. At this age, girlfriends, favourite teachers, godparents or other trusted adults are often more suitable helpers. The process from puberty through to emerging adulthood is a critical one. Soon afterwards, your new adult daughter will be leaving home. This is one of the most important steps in every person's life, and doing it with love on both sides is crucial. If this separation does not go well, there will be a lifelong dependency; we then talk of 'Mummy's boys' or 'Daddy's girls'. These young people cannot detach themselves from either their mums or their dads; they continue to be dependent on them, instead of strengthening their own ego and developing their own personality.[1]

What does puberty mean?

But let's go back to puberty first. What does it mean – and what happens in this stage of life?

The word 'puberty' comes from the Latin pubertas, meaning sexual maturity. The root of the word is related to the Latin pubes, meaning pubic hair. However, before this starts appearing, the female body is increasing its generation of the sex hormone oestrogen. This sometimes happens from the age of eight or nine. How does the body know that it is ready? Why do some girls reach puberty sooner than others? Body weight plays a significant role in this. At about 38–43 kilograms, the hormonal control system signals that it's time to begin the move into womanhood.[2]

Hormones act in a similar way to yeast or baking powder. They stimulate physical growth and help us carry out certain behaviours more easily and with more relish – nursing a baby, for example, is made possible by the action of the hormone prolactin, which causes the breasts to produce milk. Steroid hormones bring about the growth of the brain during puberty; they boost thinking and questioning. Oestrogen activates a girl's body to become rounded and to grow, to feel adult sexual pleasure and desire and to seek sexual satisfaction.

The search for personal identity

In the search for their personal identity, both girls and boys ask important questions: Who am I? How would I like to turn out? How do others see me?

During this process, girls come up against the barriers of culturally defined femininity time after time. They are constantly asked to consider others' expectations, and, where possible, to fulfil them. 'With characteristics like pleasantness, adaptability, restraint, they conform to social expectations,' writes Dörte Stolle.[3]

The pressures during puberty

It is during puberty that girls who were previously self-confident may begin to doubt their abilities and question themselves. Images of beauty that they see in the media every day show them how an attractive woman has to look, and how important it is to be attractive. They notice that it's hard to be 'a good girl' and at the same time withstand the pressures of performance and competition. That makes it difficult for insecure girls to be satisfied with their bodies. When I ask my daughter what makes girls so insecure, the first thing she mentions is magazines for women and teenagers, which many girls read. 'The magazines tell you how you should apply make-up and how to dress. And then if it doesn't look as good, you're disappointed,' she says. Eighteen-year-old Ellie writes about herself, 'Sometimes I want to be like the female Pope in the Middle Ages, who was a very courageous woman. She found her way, even through danger. But sometimes I think first about what others want of me – boys and men. Then I know I must be warm-hearted, modest, devoted, soft and adaptable, attractive, slim as well as rounded; I must have a pouting mouth, beautiful hands, not too many muscles. That's how they like it to be, I think. Because I know this, I play on it occasionally, I use it.'[4]

Adolescence is the cornerstone, the hub of girls' psychic, social and biological development. On the one hand, they experience traditional role allocation, but at the same time they also see unconventional, flexible lifestyles. They see popstars who earn millions, while their own parents cannot manage to scrape up enough for a holiday despite going off to work for eight hours a day. Finding your way in this jungle of possibilities is difficult.

Mentors

For many young women, having a mentor – an experienced contact person who can hand on her knowledge – is a great help. Such mentors can be teachers (most often from outside school – someone the girl knows through riding or piano lessons, for instance), neighbours, sports coaches or a girl's own grandmother or godparent. A mentor can also function as a mediator in the main battlefront of disagreements – the family.

The role of the peer group

During puberty, being a member of a group of girls around the same age is very important. Groups at school or in the community help girls exchange ideas and support each other. An 'us-feeling' is generated in these groups. In their group, growing girls can safely experiment with hair-dos, clothing and make-up. Telephone calls and many hours spent together help them to develop their own identity and to practise social skills. Intense friendships are common at this stage, and they serve many positive purposes: they teach girls to cope with individual weaknesses, to say no, and to become empathetic conversation partners; and they offer girls the chance to experience respect and recognition. Peer groups can also take on mentoring functions, as experiences are shared and passed on. In this life stage it is often easier to learn from contemporaries than from adults.

It can be difficult for girls and women to develop their own identity these days, especially if they don't match the current beauty image. So our daughters are under pressure in many ways. It's not always easy for them to cut the umbilical cord to their mother and develop their own personality, or to avoid conforming to stereotypes. Your daughter needs help at this time – above all, listen to her, and don't take her moods to heart.

The female cycle

With puberty, a girl enters the female cycle – and this is much more than beginning to menstruate. There are four phases of this cycle, and each has its own 'flavour'; I like to compare them with the seasons.

The first phase starts with the maturation of the egg in the follicle, which is a cell nucleus in the ovary. So that the egg can mature, the body produces the hormone oestrogen, which also activates the womb and breasts. You could compare this phase with early spring: in Earth's core, everything is already growing, even if outside it's still winter and nature seems to be sleeping. In the girl's or woman's body, possibilities are emerging ...

In the second phase, there's ovulation. A special hormone helps here, too. Between about the fourteenth and the sixteenth day of the cycle, a mature egg moves into the incubating sleeve. This phase corresponds to late spring – trees blossom, attracting insects with their colours and scents, so that they can be fertilised. This is also the 'fruitful period' of the female cycle; many women feel particular pleasure in their sexuality in this phase.

In the third phase, the egg is changed into the so-called gestagen nucleus. This generates gestagen, which is made up mostly of progesterone, a hormone that induces the womb to prepare to receive the egg. The womb's lining thickens and is enriched with nutrients. This phase corresponds to summer. The fruit is ripening, and unfertilised blossoms start to wither. There are no special hormones needed now. The egg has matured. Oestrogen and progesterone fall to their lowest levels. During this phase, girls often feel bad-tempered and aggressive or depressed. In the body, the gestagen cells and womb lining now decompose.

The womb lining detaches itself in the fourth phase, which we call menstruation. This phase corresponds to autumn. What kind of blood is it that flows out of the body? Explain its characteristics to your daughter, as this blood really deserves to be treated with respect! It contains a lot of vitamins, proteins, iron, copper, magnesium, kalium, calcium and other mineral salts, as well as a large number of immune cells.

When you understand this cycle, you can deal with mood fluctuations with more consideration. No female remains unaffected by the changes the cycle brings.

Many girls are proud when they have their first period – they know they are becoming women

First menstruation

When I had my first period, I was eleven and all alone. My mother was seriously ill and nobody had prepared me for menstruation. There were no sanitary towels, so I had to work out on my own how I could best manage my bloodied underpants. Many girls of my generation had nightmarish experiences. The women of my generation made sure they didn't repeat that behaviour. When their daughters were quite young, they showed them that they bled once a month and told them that this belongs to being a woman.

It is important that girls know that menstruation is connected to the ability to bear children. Once they appreciate this, girls can be proud when they have their first period, and make no secret of it. For them it is a reason to celebrate.

I suggest that you talk with your daughter, before she is likely to have her first period, about what she would like to do when it happens. Would she like to celebrate it in some way? This way, your daughter will at least know that you are glad she's becoming a woman. She may have her own ideas. Perhaps she would like to just go out somewhere nice to eat. Perhaps she wants to buy a symbolic gift – a ring or a chain with a special pendant, say, to signal her transition to womanhood and full femininity.

Help with menstruation pain

Today many girls reach for pain-relief tablets without hesitating, because their mothers advise them to do that. I don't think it's smart; it can lead to dependence and unnecessary drug consumption. Instead, I recommend you take up old women's teachings again. If the home remedies I suggest here don't work, visit a doctor to find out how your daughter can best manage her symptoms.

Keep an eye out for the herbs lady's mantle (of the genus Alchemilla) and yarrow (of the genus Achillea), both of which can provide effective treatment. If you have a garden, or a balcony, you could grow them. Knowing that she can help herself may make your daughter feel in control of her life, which will boost her self-esteem.

When you pick these herbs, dry them in a shaded place, then mix the two together and make a very diluted tea. This can help with menstruation pains. If you don't have an opportunity to grow these plants yourself, you can find special women's teas in health food or organic food stores. As well as this sort of remedy, your daughter will need a hot-water bottle.

Another thing that helps is massage. Make a massage oil with jojoba or almond oil, and add the following:

1 drop of essential rose oil

1 drop of Roman camomile oil

1 drop of cypress oil

2 drops of marjoram oil.

Massaged gently onto the belly, this can work miracles.

A visualisation exercise to help soothe menstruation pain

Make yourself quite comfortable with a blanket and the hot-water bottle … Close your eyes, and get used to the welcome darkness … Imagine that it is helping you to forget your everyday cares … Feel the security that the darkness is giving you … And imagine that the darkness contains everything … Look at the night sky … How dark it is … Look at the stars and galaxies, the Milky Way … Look at the moon and its glimmer … Envelop the darkness in your body … It's a source of renewal and transformation … As each night allows the new day to appear … The darkness is the source of all being … We are returning from the darkness and coming back to ourselves … Enjoy the darkness for a little while longer … And then come back here into the room … Move your hands and feet and come completely back, refreshed and awake.

Teenage pregnancy by Steve Biddulph

First of all, let's be clear that teenage pregnancy isn't bad or wrong. It's been the normal thing for the human race for most of its history. It's just that in our society, it's hard for a young couple, or a young woman on her own, to avoid poverty unless they are able to finish their education, get some qualifications, and manage the cost and time demands that a baby makes. (There have been some very welcome back-to-school programs trialled in high schools, helping young mothers to both parent well and finish their education. And remarkably, these programs have been found to reduce the pregnancy rates in those schools – it's good for other teenagers to see the reality of teen parenting face to face.) But on the whole, teenage pregnancy is a setback that in most cases you would want to avoid.

So what can you do to help your daughter avoid getting pregnant too young? It turns out that the way you live your life as a parent is the biggest factor in whether your daughter chooses to get pregnant at a very young age.

According to a study by Professor Julie Quinlivan, professor of obstetrics at Melbourne University and head of the Royal Women's Hospital's 'Young Mums' clinic, about a third of teenage mothers actually plan their pregnancies, and believe that having a baby will be one of the most positive experiences of their lives.[5]

Professor Quinlivan told the *Sydney Morning Herald* that the appeal of getting pregnant, for some girls, is in the chance to build a loving family life for themselves, which is sometimes in contrast to their own experience. She found that teenage mothers were much more likely to have come from fractured families, and so were seeking love and security through having a baby. This can be a recipe for disaster unless a lot of support is provided.

Professor Quinlivan found that more than half of the teenage mothers studied had parents who had separated before they were five years old, (that's five times higher than the normal rate). They were also ten times more likely to have been exposed to violence between their parents, and to have had negative relationships with them.

For some teenagers, creating their own family was a way to escape, Professor Quinlivan said. 'If you have an adverse early life, you want to grow up fast, and get out early to feel safer.'

One of the strongest themes to emerge from interviews with pregnant teenagers was their idealisation of motherhood – more than half expected it would be the most exciting event of their lives. (But that's true for most of the rest of us, too!) The problem lay in what made it exciting: the prospect of a baby's unconditional love. 'That comes through all the time, that this is someone who loves me,' Professor Quinlivan said.

She added that the findings showed that it was not simply a matter of improving sex education or access to contraception. Rather, it was one of 'breaking the cycle', as the children of teenage parents were more likely to become teenage parents themselves.

About two-thirds of the teenage mums Professor Quinlivan studied are doing well. 'The ones who do well have family support, get back into education, and don't have another baby straight away,' Professor Quinlivan said. About half of teenage mothers have another child within two years, which makes it difficult for them to continue their education.

So, to conclude, if you don't want your daughter to become a teenage mum:

- Make sure you and your partner are not violent to each other.
- Demonstrate respectful relationships to her.
- Give her lots of unconditional love, involvement and security.
- If you are a dad, stay around and stay involved in her life.

Some of these are a pretty hard call. If you are in a violent marriage, do you leave, and become a 'fractured family' or stay and 'model poor relationships'? Perhaps the only good answer is to get help. Because every step you manage to make towards safe, secure, involved family living will strengthen the safety net around your daughter.

And if your daughter does become pregnant? Then, the support of others to continue her schooling and settle in well with her new baby (and hopefully her partner) is essential to things working out. After all, a baby is a gift, even if the timing isn't great.

The importance of staying connected

As long as you stay connected with your daughter during adolescence, you won't lose her. This is old knowledge and common sense, but you'll see it confirmed again and again. The quality of your conversations with her will decide how well or badly your relationship will proceed.

I would like to suggest some rules that may improve your communication with your pubescent daughter:

- Talk about yourself in 'I' sentences. It doesn't matter how passionate you feel – if you stay with this approach, you won't go wrong. For example, say, 'The mess in this room upsets me!', or 'I'm so angry I can't talk.' Avoid 'you' sentences like, 'You're scruffy and unsociable!' This way, your daughter has no chance of contradicting anything you say.

- Don't use generalisations; if you do, your daughter will have no chance of escaping the accusation. And in truth, no-one is always 'unfriendly, filthy and uninterested'. And not 'everything' is irritating, too hard or boring. Reproaches that are put this way, even if they are valid at the time, discourage your daughter. How can she ever live up to your expectations if she 'always' does 'everything' wrong? When you speak in generalisations, you don't allow any exceptions. Instead, try to talk about specific things: 'You've forgotten to take out your plate', or 'What didn't you like about the play? The last time we went to one you were quite keen', or 'When you rolled your eyes, I was disappointed. Let's talk more about this tomorrow.'

- Deal with specific situations: 'No, it's not all right for you to turn on the TV now. We agreed you'd do your homework first', or 'The guinea pigs' cage is still dirty. Please clean it now.'

- Take her feelings seriously and express what you notice about them: 'I can see that you're sad. What's happened?', or 'I can see that that makes you mad. Do you want to talk about it?', or 'Obviously, you're bored. If you're interested, I'd suggest …'

- Every person has the right to their own feelings, and your daughter has the right to express hers, just as you have a right to express yours. We all share our feelings. Accept a feeling your daughter expresses as a request for something to be discussed later. Passionate feelings require a cooling-off period before their causes can be talked about.

- Pay your daughter compliments frequently. In families where people feel good, there will generally be about one critical comment for every five positive ones. See how your family rates on this scale, and try to reach that one in five ratio.

There are lots of statements and comments that always have a negative effect on relationships. Because we've heard such comments from our parents, teachers and others, we use them ourselves, unfortunately. Check your own vocabulary for the following conversation and self-esteem killers. If you do use them, try not to:

- What is the matter with you?
- How often do I have to tell you?
- Can't you do anything right?
- You're a clumsy fool!
- Typical girl!
- Let me do it – you can't.
- If you do that, you'll …
- Just look at this mess. It's all yours …
- What on earth do you have on?
- How will you ever …?
- Just have a look at how many mistakes you've made!

If you want to know how positive conversations between adults and children run, read the therapeutic stories of Doris Brett (see the bibliography).

Loosening the leash

Young people know that family is very important. It moulds them, gives them security, and is the place where they can deal with conflicts and build a life. But adolescence can be a testing time for everyone.

You might be surprised at how, suddenly, your daughter will insist on being allowed to do this or that – parties, films, cigarettes, discos, solariums, alcohol, music festivals, visits from and to boys, travelling, certain clothing. You'll constantly be badgered with the question, 'Mum, can I …? Dad, can I …?' If you say yes, you'll probably die of anxiety, and if you say no, a volcano erupts.

Giving her some freedom

Some parents keep their children on a short leash. These young people stay at home longer and fit in with their parents' expectations. They sometimes find a place where they can get away from their parents and exercise a little personal freedom in sports clubs or youth groups. But if the parents' style of upbringing is too strict, young people often react with resistance or evasive behaviour.

An upbringing where children have a reasonable amount of freedom gives them room to grow into who they want to be.[6] Young people raised this way tend to value good conversation, have less trouble separating from their parents, and can critically analyse social conventions. But it's unwise to loosen the leash too much, as excessive freedom can be just as dangerous as excessive control – as we will see later in the chapter.

If you think your daughter is lazy, talk to her about it, don't put her on trial!

Handing over responsibility

The challenge for you as a parent is to be present and communicative with your children, and at the same time to gradually hand over responsibility to them as they grow up. This makes their separation from you as smooth as possible.

Once your daughter reaches puberty, you cannot continue to bring her up the way you did when she was small. It's more a case of walking beside her and constantly staying in dialogue with her. Mind you, you can only rarely 'set up' important conversations. It is better to wait attentively for the right moment. Usually, deep and meaningful talks just happen – during car trips, at a sick bed, during a cuppa together or in some other daily situation. If you don't take these opportunities when they arise, or always say that you have 'no time', you'll waste most of your chances.

I will not advise you about what you should and should not allow your daughter to do. As parents, you must decide that and accept responsibility for that yourselves. One thing is sure, though: you must know what your position is, and be able to justify it. You daughter needs your advice and your perspective. However, whether she does what you recommend or not is another matter. Don't be surprised if she occasionally contradicts you – that's completely normal. She must learn to find her own way and test herself, and words are one way she will do that.

'Puberty is a period of unbelievably big egotism, narcissism and uncertainty,' writes Margot Kässmann.[7] 'It seems to me that young people are so preoccupied with themselves that they don't really manage to notice others deeply. I suppose parents have to expect that the seed they planted in earlier years will bear fruit – that's what it's about – but it can take a long time.' So don't agonise over every outbreak of temper or be too judgemental in general. And always allow yourselves to be convinced by a good excuse.

If you say no too often, you run the risk of being lied to; but if you allow everything, she'll be open to unnecessary risks

Strict or lax

Talk to other parents, and listen to them too. You will think that some behave too rigidly during their daughter's adolescence, and that others are too lax. Take a couple of examples such as all-day outdoor music festivals and discos. I only allowed them from the age of sixteen; that seemed sensible to me. But even with that, exceptions can sometimes be appropriate. For example, if your daughter is particularly responsible, or has an elder brother with her, or is accompanied by the parents of a girlfriend, then perhaps fifteen is fine. If you forbid too much, there's a risk you will be lied to or that your daughter will rebel. My advice is to keep talking with her. Tell her your opinions, your concerns and fears, but make sure you listen well when she answers you – it's worth it!

Setting limits, showing trust by Steve Biddulph

The aim of parenthood is that one day your children will be adults who can handle the real world. They will know for themselves when to say no to another drink, when to leave a situation where they are in sexual or physical danger, when they need sleep, and when to eat nourishing food. They will know how to balance work and play, how to differentiate friendship from lust, and how to separate loyalty from being used. But these are complicated things, which even we adults have trouble with! So nature allows ten years to learn them, and those years are called adolescence.

The job of the parent of an adolescent is to give young people the thinking tools to be able to do this. Which involves a gradual process, trial and error, and lots of talking.

Parents get limit-setting wrong when they go too far towards freedom or too far towards restriction. Here are two stories that show what can go wrong:

David and Ellie held a party for their fifteen-year-old daughter, a student at an expensive private school. They figured this age group liked their own space, so they didn't supervise, but stayed upstairs in their 'retreat' part of the house. So they didn't notice when one of their daughter's friends collapsed on the front median strip at 1 a.m. from alcohol poisoning, and went into a coma that lasted for sixteen hours in intensive care, causing a nightmare of anxiety and danger for all concerned that she would emerge unscathed.

Patrick and Angelina took the other approach, never letting their seventeen-year-old daughter go to parties for fear of drugs, not letting her go out to friends' houses, and fretting over her diet, her clothes, her homework. When friends actually visited, Patrick and Angelina plied them with scones and cream, hovered anxiously about, and tried to engage them in conversations that soon had them fleeing, never to return. When their daughter was eighteen, she ran away from home with an unemployed drummer and was pregnant within three months. They didn't see her for two years.

These sorts of horror stories might make you decide that some kind of 'middle road' is what you need to take. But it's not only that, since everyone thinks they are already taking a middle road. You have to have a strategy for building self-sufficiency in your daughter, gradually and in a way that fits her age and stage.

Some guidelines:

- Girls are not mature enough to handle sexual pressures (their own, or those of boys) until aged at least 16 or 17, and sometimes not even then. So unsupervised parties, being in mixed groups without adults around, being out and about with friends without a general purpose (such as to go shopping and home again, to go to a sports game with a girlfriend, and back straight after) should be approached with a lot of care.
- Trust isn't the same as wishful thinking. It's based on experience …

    … 'We trusted you to be home from your friends at 11.00 on Friday night, and you did that just fine. So you can go there again this week.'

… 'You said you'd get a ride home from netball with Jenny's mum, but you came with her brother driving you instead. That's not what we agreed. If you want to go to her house this weekend, you have to phone us, and we'll come and get you. It's a long way, so you can pay us back by cooking tea one night next week.'

… 'If you work really hard to help keep the house and your room clean this week, and cook tea one night during the week, it'll help me feel less like the maid around here. Then we can talk some more about your idea to have a sleepover with your girlfriends.'

The idea is very clear, and as old as time. Freedom is something you earn. Don't be too cold and mechanical about it, it's a friendly and light-hearted thing, but a real one all the same. Adults are people who pull their weight. Teenagers are people who are learning to. The message to send them is: the more responsible you can be, the more responsibility you can have. And even then, be mindful that this is still a young person you are dealing with, prone to misjudging or overestimating herself. Do it in baby steps.

- When something goes wrong, talk about it with 'I-statements' rather than attacks and blame …

… 'I was scared and couldn't sleep. I didn't know if I should ring the police. You are really precious to me. I don't want to go through that again. I need you to always phone if you get into trouble.'

… 'I was embarrassed when you swore when we were talking with your grade six teacher. I want you to notice where you are and who you are with, and choose what comes out of your mouth.'

- 'Hassling' – the process of sorting these things out – is a routine part of adolescence. Be good-natured about it, and don't take it personally. It means they are on track. Their frontal cortex is growing at this stage, and teenagers can be unbelievably stupid at times, and by discussing and even arguing, as long as its not too heated, they can begin to program rational thought back into their brains.

- It helps if they know you love them. Watch the ratio of serious and fun, criticism and praise, warmth and sternness. The aim is for your daughter to feel that you like her, you have fun times together daily on the least pretext – turning up the radio when a good song comes on, and leaping about the kitchen, joking, sharing a hug on the couch, talking about your lives. Some families are just so serious all the time – schedules, homework, ballet lessons, parents' worries, work – that it's enough to depress any teenager.

If you are very stressed by your own life, or theirs, you are likely to make matters worse, and a counsellor can sometimes help – they can give you emotional support and a sense of perspective. Even better are friends to talk with and compare notes. But the very best thing is to slow your life down, ditch some responsibilities and commitments, so that when the unexpected comes along, you have some reserves of calm, it's not the 'last straw'. After toddlerhood, the early to mid-teens are the years of greatest need for guidance in a girl's childhood, and you have to be available and committed. Adolescence is not the time to take a back seat.

But it can be fun, and the reward is a fantastically capable young adult.

Staying on track

At the onset of puberty, a number of girls start to let their school marks slide. This is understandable if you consider what drastic physical and emotional changes they're going through. Patience and understanding are what these girls need; punishment and pressure will only drive them into a corner. Remember, many a girl has taken her own life because her school achievements did not satisfy her parents. More boys than girls kill themselves, but all parents need to take these numbers seriously. It is during puberty that your daughter may need you most – and if she has trouble at school, you must stand by her.

Children must take responsibility for tasks, but it has to happen step by step. Make it a rule that if your daughter doesn't finish her jobs, she can't claim privileges. 'You may go to the movies – but your homework must be done beforehand'; 'I'll drive you to your girlfriend's if you clean your aquarium first.' If you don't get anywhere with this kind of bargaining and the situation gets nasty, you'll need support. Talk with your partner, with your daughter's teachers, with other parents, or with a therapist. Sometimes an outsider can see what is going on more clearly than you can, and can contribute to solutions.

For lots of teenage girls, school is primarily the place where they meet their girlfriends and interesting boys. If there's a good atmosphere in the school and students can speak openly to their teachers and among themselves, they will also take on challenging tasks. Look at the enormous commitment young people display when they're preparing for a school performance or running a fundraising project, for example.

Some common adolescent crises

Growing into the adult world is the most difficult phase in life. It should not surprise anyone that many young people experience some sort of crisis during this period. However, many problems can be overcome through dialogue – with parents, friends, godparents and others.

Girls need strong parents during this period, but 'strong' as in parents who know what their beliefs are and stick to them, not 'strong' as in bossy. Your daughter should know what you believe, and how strongly you will stick to your beliefs – even if they are different from hers – but she should also know that you will never leave her in the lurch, even when she makes mistakes. You and your daughter can only talk to each other really honestly if there is this level of trust and understanding between you.

Try to remember that crises are always opportunities. When a young girl has her hair dyed blue, and/or seems angry all the time, and/or is rude constantly, and/or has poor school marks, and/or commits robberies, and/or suffers anorexia nervosa … and there are many other things we could add to this list … she will shake up the whole family. It may be very difficult at times to see it, and to feel like acting on it, but all these behaviours are an opportunity for change.

Family therapy, which is one approach to this sort of crisis, doesn't just help the girl; it helps the whole family. Everyone is a winner when individual circumstances are recognised, secrets aired or complicated situations clarified. After a crisis has been successfully overcome, the family relationships are generally more mature, deeper and more affectionate.

There are three particular crises that more and more girls are experiencing: eating disorders, drugs and depression.

Eating disorders

It is mainly girls who suffer from eating disorders such as anorexia nervosa (where they stop eating) or bulimia (where food is eaten but then deliberately regurgitated).

It is obvious that eating disorders can only occur in countries where there's enough money and food for everyone to eat their fill. At the same time, in these countries, which are basically the Western industrialised nations, many children now miss out on some of the natural ways of being looked after: they spend less time altogether – and less peaceful, relaxed time – with their parents. Many of us live under great pressure. We feel obliged to perform to high standards and are constantly stressed. In our world, it's easy enough to forget that children need simple things: they need to feel they belong and are understood, and for this to happen, you need to spend time with them.

In her book on girls' developmental crises, psychiatrist Dörte Stolle tells the story of Carina, a young girl who suffered from anorexia nervosa. At the age of fifteen, Carina believed that her little brother was her mother's favourite, and that she didn't get enough attention. She rarely saw her father, whom she loved. On the one hand, Carina felt stretched too far, as a kind of partner for her mother, and on the other hand, as a child, she felt too restricted. She wanted more autonomy, so she stopped eating – but that led to any autonomy she had being removed. Her life was at risk: she was 168 cm tall and weighed only 44 kilograms, and was then admitted to a youth psychiatric ward.

With the help of one-on-one conversation, occupational therapy and hypnotherapy, Carina finally succeeded in freeing herself from the illness. She wrote about herself, 'My parents were no role models for me. They didn't understand me at all, but always behaved as if everything was all right. In previous years, my father was always away on business; often we only saw each other at weekends. I think my mother wanted to replace him, and she tried to present a harmonious family life to the outside world, but she was not happy, not even satisfied. I somehow had the feeling that I should have helped her. Sometimes, I thought I was not even her daughter, but her partner.'[8]

Differences of opinion are normal during puberty – but does your daughter feel totally misunderstood? Does she feel that she has to help you out or somehow be your partner? If you suspect that she does, warning lights should come on: it's time to do something about it. Try family therapy – before your daughter gets into a life-threatening crisis.

Don't tune out

If you listen to your daughter right from the beginning, and if everyone in the family can openly express their feelings, the whole family can find better ways of living together. Children are fundamentally cooperative, and they sometimes hide their true feelings if they think their parents could be upset by them. Carina never said to her father, 'Dad, please stay here, I need you!' And she probably did not show her anger about her little brother either, because she wanted to be the good girl.

Attentive parents could have seen from her behaviour before she stopped eating that Carina was not doing well – and taken steps to find out what the problems were and solve them. If your daughter is one of those people who shout out their feelings uninhibitedly, be grateful, not alarmed. It's a superb survival technique! And think about it: perhaps there are messages there for your own behaviour.

There are three particular crises that more and more girls are experiencing: eating disorders, drugs and depression

Drugs and alcohol

Lisa also felt misunderstood by her parents; she began to consume alcohol regularly at the age of thirteen. She rebelled against her parents, who reacted with punishment, severity and control. 'You'll end up on the streets!' her father predicted. He was the classic accuser, someone who found fault in everything. Her mother was the exact opposite: she tried to sweep problems under the carpet, and looked away when Lisa drank. The façade – that everything was just fine – had to be kept intact, after all.

Lisa felt torn between her parents. Her mother was no role model because she had too little backbone and no opinion of her own. Her father would have been a better role model, because he at least had opinions and expressed them, but she hated him because he mocked her and punished her for every little thing (as she saw it).

After a session of family therapy, both parents managed to improve their own behaviour as individuals and as a couple. Lisa's father then gave her more space, but still demanded that she follow certain rules – not to drink alcohol, primarily. He also finally gave her some positive attention and time: he drove her to functions, and became more supportive generally. The relationship between them improved, and they could talk normally again. Lisa's mother expressed her opinions more often and showed Lisa that she did have her own aims and interests; however, she supported her husband when he insisted that Lisa stick to the rules the three of them agreed on.

On her fourteenth birthday, Lisa was permitted to have a party – without alcohol and cigarettes, but with loud music.

During puberty, many girls will resort to drugs, alcohol and cigarettes. As parents, you will not be able to fully prevent this, but what you can do is lead the way by setting a good example and expressing your opinion. The message you need to convey to your teenage daughter is: 'We're here for you and will stand by you, even if you do something wrong. Let's work out, together, how we can repair the damage.'

Depression

There are several common causes of adolescent depression – the break-up of a friendship, the death or serious illness of a family member, stress and failure at school, and rejection by someone the teenager loves. Any of these can lead to depression, sometimes even to suicide. Depression is also often associated with anxiety. As parents, you should take the first signs of depression very seriously.

So how do you know if your daughter is clinically depressed? According to the DSM-IV (a directory of all known mental illnesses), the signs that indicate someone may have clinical depression are as follows:

- depressed or irritable mood
- diminished interest or pleasure in most activities
- significant change in weight or appetite
- insomnia or hypersomnia
- fatigue or loss of energy
- feelings of worthlessness or guilt
- impaired thinking, concentration or decision-making
- thoughts of not being here any more.[9]

If your daughter has five or more of these symptoms for two weeks continuously, there is a possibility that she is suffering from a depressive illness.

Girls suffering from depression seldom reveal it explicitly to others. They tend to have few or no girlfriends, and often withdraw into themselves. Sometimes a pet, such as a dog or a horse, can be of great help. If you have a good, open relationship with your daughter, understanding chats that offer solutions and convey hope and trust can also help. However, if you are at all concerned, get some therapeutic assistance.

There are many ways in which medical facilities can help depressed girls; they do it every day. However, your daughter must first agree to get some help. The person you speak to first may herself be able to assist you in helping and supporting your daughter, and will definitely be able to explain the types of treatment that are available and help you work out which might be most suitable for your daughter.

Self-defence and its benefits

We live in a world full of violence and struggle. As a rule, we women have not learned to fight for ourselves – this must change. Self-defence courses help us become tougher and get a good sense of our physical capability and strength. They also help us on other levels: they teach us that women and girls are allowed to assert themselves, occupy a space and defend their positions and views. So self-defence is not only about physical ability; it's also a mental stance that says, 'I'm allowed to put up a fight!'

Help your daughter to feel joy in physical movement and expression, and encourage her to treat her body like a temple!

Find out what courses there are in your area. Aikido, judo and karate are combat sports that strengthen your whole body; they also teach you respect for your opponent. When you bow to your opponent, as you do before and after each bout, you are expressing your respect for them. After all, it is only through and with an opponent that you can learn and progress.

There are also short self-defence courses that teach you special tactics that you can apply straight away, without years of training.

The difference physical self-confidence can make

Nicky Marone tells a true story about 21-year-old Ginny, who worked nights in a restaurant. She was a small and dainty woman, and was always afraid of walking to her car at night after work. One night, she noticed a man close to her car. She feared he wanted to do something to her. She was terribly frightened, but decided to muster all her courage and defend herself. First she threw her handbag to the ground, then she took up a self-defence position, feet braced wide apart, her weight evenly balanced, fists held up. She yelled, 'Hey, you. I don't know what you want or why you're here, but I'm telling you, it's not going to be easy for you! I'm ready for you!'

For a few moments, they faced each other. Then the man turned away and went off, without turning around. Ginny attributes her ability to carry out this action to her father. She was a second child, and had been expected to be a boy; her father took her fishing and hunting, practised arm-wrestles with her and showed her how to repair cars. Through all this, she somehow identified with male behaviour patterns. Marone writes, 'Ginny would most likely have become a victim had she not learned how to behave aggressively. Regrettably, aggressive behaviour is not encouraged for women.'[10]

In a nutshell

- Teach your daughter about the physical changes that accompany the onset of puberty, and explain that surprising emotional changes can also occur.

- Be open about discussing menstruation, and treat it as something to celebrate – your daughter is becoming a woman – rather than a 'curse'.

- It is vital to stay connected with your daughter as she moves into her teens.

- Striking the right balance between freedom and restriction of her activities will help her through these tricky years.

- Beware the three main pitfalls for adolescent girls: eating disorders, drugs and alcohol, and depression.

- Acquiring some self-defence skills can help your daughter's self-confidence as well as her physical safety.

The power of the maternal instinct

May (4 years), Cristina (7) and I – their mother – were out walking in the bush one beautiful winter's day. I had for some time been thinking, as a mum, about safety, control, independence and letting go. I watched my gorgeous girls roam and play, laugh and banter, and I decided to let go of all those thoughts and just enjoy the day. We were on our way to Turtle Creek to see if we could spot any.

'Let's run!' Cristina suggests when we get closer to a bridge crossing the creek. May doesn't need any more encouragement than that and heads off. Within minutes we reach the bridge, out

of breath. It has recently rained – everything is wet, green and sparkling. The creek is full of water that is very muddy after the rain. I feel happy and blessed with all this beauty.

May steps up onto a log running along the edge of the bridge. I open my mouth to tell her to step down, but I am way too late. All I see is a little green arm vanish into the muddy waters several metres below us. Before I can give any rational thought to my actions, I scream, quickly scan the banks – which are completely impenetrable with lantana – and pull off my boots and my thick woolly jumper. I have no conscious thought of this, and am later surprised to find the jumper on the bridge.

I look down – no sign of May. I crawl down the side of the bridge to find a spot I can jump from, well away from where May fell in so I don't land on her. I feel very strong. I swing out and let go. Thankfully, there is nothing but water under me when I land – no rocks, no logs, and no May.

No May! Where is she? I start to panic. The worst-case scenario runs through my brain like a wild and hellish nightmare. I can't go underwater to look for her because there is no visibility. I start to feel around in the water with my hands in the hope of finding an arm or a leg … anything to drag her up by. My heart is pounding and I have started to dry sob. I do not want to go through the grief of losing a child. I don't want to … I don't want to … I don't want to …

Suddenly I feel something other than water running through my fingers. I grab hold of it and in a second my life changes again. Spluttering and coughing and crying, May is in my arms. I hug her and hug her, probably squeezing the remaining water out of her lungs. She is here, she is back, she is alive!

How we got out of the creek and back home is a mystery to me – I remember nothing of it. What I do remember, though, is Cristina looking up at me with big, blue, laughing eyes and saying, 'Mum, you swung off that bridge like a monkey!'

Micky

Sticking to boundaries

One of the most difficult things to do is to set boundaries, which are essential for both the parent and the child. Fifteen can be a difficult age, and when one of my daughters was this age she had the ability to 'press my buttons'. I tended to respond in a very negative way.

One evening we had such a confrontation – I now cannot remember what it was about. It was as though there was no thought or acceptance on her part that I also had needs and rights. I felt so angry with her that I told her I could imagine pushing her down the stairs. I felt this was an horrific thing to say, let alone to imagine the actual act. She did not seem to be the least perturbed, and merely stated that I had to take her to school at 7 a.m. I told her to catch the bus.

The next morning it was dark and raining. As I went past the bus stop with the dog on my usual walk, my daughter said, 'I missed the bus. You'll go back and get the car and take me to school, won't you Mummy?'

I again said no. I ran off only to stop around the corner, sit on the side of the road and have a good cry. Things seemed better between us after that, but what is very interesting is that she does not even remember that incident, and yet for me it was pivotal in the change in our relationship.

She is now the most amazing young woman who I love to spend time with. Recently she sent me a text message to tell me that I was fantastic! The feeling is mutual.

Delwyn

EIGHT

RELATIONSHIPS IN THE FAMILY

Mother–daughter relationships are different to father–daughter relationships. Both are close, ideally, but they serve different purposes in a girl's development.

The relationship between a mother and her daughter is unique and intense. The Russian *matrioshkas* – the colourful dolls within dolls within dolls – clearly represent this close relationship: over generations, one woman emerges from the other.

Most mums and daughters have a strong relationship from the very beginning – due in part to the simple biological fact that the mum personally experiences the nine months of pregnancy. Many fathers have told me that their baby became 'real' for them at the precise moment of birth; for other dads, a strong bond with their daughter was not instant, but has grown beautifully over time.

Mothers and daughters

Mother–daughter relationships are not always good. The relationship of the mother to her own mother plays a role in this.

Sociologist Marianne Krüll gives us an example of how this relationship can affect the next generation: 'My mother treated her mother condescendingly and scornfully. I learned, through her, that it is normal for a daughter to scorn her mother. My mother provided me with a model for this, so the way she handled her own mother was the way I behaved towards her twenty years later.'[1]

Sometimes, a mother who feels she had a raw deal in her education or in her career or job – and she may well be right, of course – will push her daughter to do whatever it was she herself missed out on. With the best of intentions, an expectation is placed upon the daughter that does not match the girl's own needs: a girl who would far prefer to play football may be forced to learn piano or take ballet lessons. These daughters might feel as if they are living in a straitjacket, and often they will take a big, painful swing at freedom later on.

A mother whose own mother could only give her a little or no love will sometimes find it hard to be loving herself. These mothers could be called 'unnatural mothers'. However, this is a little unfair, because in such cases there was always an 'unnatural child', too – a child who was neglected. If the entanglement and pain stay hidden below the surface, unacknowledged and not dealt with, the unkind or ill-treating mode of behaviour will be handed down from generation to generation. If the mother can clarify her own feelings and wishes in therapy, or through some other method, and begin to find a new, healing pathway, the cycle can be broken.

In discussions with mothers about their daughters, I have detected a lot of hatred and jealousy. If you feel that you simply can't get through to your daughter, and you puzzle over her behaviour, it might be useful to have a look at your own mother–daughter relationship. Find a therapist – do a little investigating, and choose the style of therapy you feel most comfortable with, and a person you trust. After all, we are living in a time and a place where the possibility of healing exists.

Examining the burdens you bring with you into motherhood and doing what you need to do to start healing – mourning and acknowledging losses are often what is needed – can sometimes really help you see your child through different eyes. It might be a good idea for you and your daughter to play or paint together. Your daughter would then have the chance to express her feelings and work through them in play or pictures. Fairytales and stories can also help. The end result of this sort of process should be that you give up the idea that your child must be the way you want her to be. If this idea is baggage from your own childhood, it may very well be because this was the approach taken by your own mother.

If instead of these sorts of difficulties you simply feel a deep, clear connection to and love for your daughter, you will probably have a harmonious and problem-free time and solve your small, everyday conflicts with humour and sympathy – at least until she hits puberty.

A family history lesson

Tell your daughter about the women in her family – her mother, aunts, cousins, grandmothers, great-grandmothers – as far back as you can. Find out what these women accomplished in great and small things. 'I remember so much of what my grandmother told me in the kitchen,' says my friend Angela. 'She had a close bond with nature, grew her own vegetables, and knew a lot about nutrition.' I think it's important to keep this kind of female wisdom alive in times of fast food giants and media-created stars. It's important for your daughter to understand that, historically, women have been keepers of much knowledge and many essential skills. Just think of all the beautiful handicrafts produced by women in the past, how they knitted, crocheted, sewed clothes and made lace – as well as cooked, washed, cleaned and more. What do you know about these skills? Which of these skills do you have? And then, of course, there are the female forebears who have worked outside the home, earning a living – which until recent times took courage and an intrepid spirit, and involved breaking down barriers and stereotypes.

What have the women in you and your daughter's history handed down to you both? It might even be worthwhile to visit a museum with your daughter to find out more, and to refresh some memories.

The power of ancestors

Your past can give you power. Just imagine all the women who have lived before you in your family standing behind you and giving you their blessing. What support that is!

Your daughter sees you as an example, every day. You're in a position to observe the differences between you and her carefully. By respecting her, paying attention to her and valuing her as a unique person, you will help your daughter develop all her gifts and talents.

In many families, people do not talk much about those who have died. Following generations of the family can suffer under this kind of family secret until someone stumbles onto it. If you come across banished, forgotten or unmourned members of the family in your family history, investigate them. It can also be helpful to draw up a family tree or write some kind of family memoir in order to give these people a suitable place in your family's heart.

Gina and Lisa: a troubled relationship

Gina is a gentle person who dresses tastefully and looks well groomed. She has had problems with her daughter Lisa, now seven, from the start. 'She was a crying baby,' she tells me, 'she wasn't happy with anything.'

Gina seems to think that even as an infant her daughter wanted to pester or challenge her parents. Lisa's father is self-employed and works very hard; he has to work in the evenings sometimes too. So during the day, Gina was almost always alone with Lisa when she was little, and she became more and more angry with this screaming creature. Little Lisa sensed this disapproval, and felt rejected and not welcomed. In her panic, she screamed louder. 'It went as far as vomiting,' says Gina. 'As a two-year-old, she stood there and yelled until she threw up.'

Now Gina has problems with Lisa's schoolwork. Lisa refuses to do homework and doesn't like to do assignments. 'She's unhappy about everything!' says her mother. 'When I go shopping for her, she always wants more.'

Lisa is fighting for her right to exist. She is deeply insecure; she doesn't yet feel that she is loved. The simplest way to show a child love is by spending time with that child, listening and talking and observing. It is senseless to criticise a child before you have a functioning relationship with her. In Lisa's case, criticism about her behaviour at school and her homework will just make her behave worse.

After a discussion with Lisa's teacher, Gina managed to totally ignore Lisa's schoolwork for a while, and instead worked on improving her relationship with Lisa. For example, they started having afternoon tea together, and using that time to talk about how they felt about things – this little routine opened new doors and created some trust.

However, the relationship between mother and daughter was obviously troubled from the start. Perhaps the birth had been very difficult, or perhaps Gina did not really want the child, and the baby felt this displeasure.

Although Gina makes sure she is involved in Lisa's school, and makes sure her daughter wants for nothing in a material sense, both of them remain unable to foster a firm bond or trusting relationship. They don't trust their love, but do not admit this to themselves.

If something is to change in all this, Gina and her mother, both of them grown-up women, should first of all look at their family. What does Gina bring from the family that is now having such negative effects? What happened to Gina's mother and grandmother? Who was not looked after? What has been kept quiet? Who was not mourned? What steps towards healing are possible?

Weighing heavily on the story of Gina and Lisa is the fact that Lisa's dad, who could have such a positive influence, is so seldom home. She is being robbed of the chance to have positive experiences with men.

Tessa and Nina: loving a daughter unconditionally

Tessa's title for her story about her daughter Nina is 'The great surprise'. 'She was so different from me, right from the start. At birth, she emitted a powerful cry – and right then I knew that she would be strong one day.'

Tessa is a reserved, uncomplicated woman. She places little value on externals, so she was especially surprised when her daughter, at the age of three, was already changing her clothes several times a day. And when Nina discovered nail polish at a girlfriend's place she went crazy for it. 'At four years of age she wanted genuine leather shoes. She certainly didn't get that from me!' explains Tessa. 'And another thing,' she says, astounded. 'My daughter always says what she wants – and then insists on carrying it through. It's exhausting, but I admire her for it.' Tessa is quite different from her daughter, but she can accept Nina the way she is – and learn from her.

This attitude facilitates a good relationship. Like every mother, Tessa cherishes a wish for Nina, an expectation: 'Nina will be strong someday.' This hope does not have a negative effect, though, because there's no disapproval behind it – it is a positive statement through and through. Her attentive manner, and a certain curiosity about her daughter, allows Tessa to love Nina unconditionally – and that's the best prerequisite for a happy relationship between mother and daughter.

The father is the first man in the life of his daughter, and therefore has particular responsibilities

Fathers and daughters

The father is the first man in the life of a little girl, and he plays an important role. He represents the masculine, the fascinating 'other', and thus is a role model. Daughters will compare every man who plays a part in their life with their father.

If you (the father) and your daughter have a very close, good relationship, she will probably choose a husband who is like you – but some daughters choose a contrasting type, because they seek a challenge. Equally, every woman who has had bad experiences with her father will look for a man who is 'quite different' – not all succeed, of course, and some of these women find themselves repeating patterns of behaviour they learned in childhood.

As with mother–daughter relationships, if the issues in strained father–daughter relationships are not worked through and entanglements are not resolved, problems will be passed from generation to generation. We know, for example, that maltreated girls often enter marriages in which they and/or their daughters are abused.

The 'positive father complex' (see page 18) is happening when girls admire and love their father above all else, adapt themselves to him happily and do lots of things for his sake. And in return, these fathers are very proud of their daughters and encourage them all the time. It is important at this point to remember that detachment occurs during puberty, and that it is essential. If it doesn't happen, the daughter will spend her whole life adapting to men, and will not develop her own identity. The self-esteem of this kind of woman will depend entirely on the extent to which she can win the admiration of men. You can easily picture the drama that occurs when such a daughter loses her father, or such a woman loses her husband.

The woman who did not experience constant parental love – ideally, from both father and mother – in her childhood, on the other hand, is deeply wounded in her self-esteem. This kind of woman, who does not feel herself worthy of love, will spend her life unconsciously offering herself as a victim, because she believes that she doesn't 'deserve' any better.

My father

My father certainly shaped me. He was a kind person who always gave his children the feeling that we were wanted and that we had all kinds of abilities and talents. And he spent a lot of time with us. When I asked myself why he was such a loving father, I remembered that he lost his own father very early. He wanted us to have lots of memories of him (and of course he wanted not to die early!). Also, he grew up among girls, so maybe he took on various female behaviours – or at least was comfortable with and understood women and girls better than many other boys. And there was perhaps a third factor: he never had to go to war.

These days, many fathers understand that they play a decisive role in their children's lives. Recently, I read with amusement something in a magazine: even perfume manufacturers are now reviewing the new masculine image. They believe that men don't need to prove their masculinity any more, and that their social focus has changed – they are more involved at home, with the family. Maybe that's why they smell a little more feminine now too!

Types of father

Do you know what type of father you are?[2]

The authoritarian father

This type believes that his wife must subordinate herself to him. You don't require a prophetic gift to see that with this type of father there's a risk that the daughter will see herself as a 'victim'. If she doesn't have a gutsy, rebellious mother, she may find it difficult to resist men with bad intentions.

If you recognise yourself here, ask yourself seriously whether it's really such a good idea for the women in your family to just do as you tell them. Wouldn't it be better for your daughter – and indeed for you – if she were allowed to make many decisions herself? The two of you would probably be closer, for a start, and your daughter would also learn that she can assert herself on her own, with commitment, intelligence and skill.

The soft father

This type is adored by his daughter. At the same time, she will manipulate him: 'If Mum says no, maybe I can still get a yes out of Dad …'. There's a danger that this daughter will learn to manipulate male behaviour using 'female cunning'. In later life, she is likely to experience many disappointments as she learns that not all men will cave in to her, and that the lowered eyes and tears do not always work.

The soft father is a good father if he shows his daughter that there are rules and limits, and that Mum and Dad will not let themselves be played off against each other. A father who displays his emotional side to his daughter will help her develop a lot of trust in him – she is likely to demonstrate this by asking him for advice later in her life.

If you fit into this category, remember to show your daughter that it's worth approaching some matters with arguments rather than emotions.

The true father by Steve Biddulph

A true father is much more than a friend. His love and his involvement with his daughter is unshakeable – whatever happens, he will be there for her, as long as he lives. So he has to be kinder, and more forgiving, than any friend would possibly be. Also, to do his job, a father has to sometimes be tougher than any friend would risk being.

There will be times when a daughter will really not like what her father says, or what he insists on. A true father expects and teaches his daughter to be a cooperative member of the family, to keep her agreements, treat others with respect, be thoughtful and pull her weight with the family's tasks of daily living. Toughness is not the same, though, as meanness. He will do the above with a quiet strength, good humoured, not attacking or ever intimidating her. It's a respectful relationship, but not, for many years, an equal one.

Deep down, this is exactly what children, including teenagers, need from their parents – the security that comes from knowing they do stand firm and can't be manipulated.

It's only by pushing against this firmness, the reasoning and ethics that a parent holds to, that teenagers learn to be strong in and with themselves. Gradually, and sometimes at a surprisingly young age, your daughter will argue with you and win. You will (if you are honest with yourself) find yourself thinking, 'I guess she's right!' At this point you can either feel miffed, or else proud that you have taught her so well. (I once heard a father at a barbecue say to his teenage daughter, when a discussion became heated, 'I don't agree with you, but I think you have great passion and good arguments.' Both father and daughter were aware of other people listening in, and she glowed with pride.)

Much of good fatherhood is in the little things – driving her to netball and watching from the sidelines, to comfort or cheer. Knowing her friends' names and meeting their parents. Helping her find a good photo of Kakadu National Park on the Internet at 10.30 at night while she desperately writes out her assignment due in tomorrow.

If you can work with her cooperatively and good naturedly on things (putting together an assemble-at-home piece of furniture, for example!) without getting tense and angry, then you are laying down the foundations for how she will do this kind of thing with her partner when she grows up. More importantly still, you will be setting the standard for the kind of partner she will choose. If you are remote, she may well choose a remote partner. If you are weak, a weak partner. If you are stressed, a stressed partner. Which is a pretty good reason to work on getting along.

Only a fraction of the time should be spent in conflict – but that time needs to be done really well. If you are able to say 'no' to your daughter, kindly, and with good reasons and no rejection, she will learn how to say 'no', when she needs to, with her peers and others. You can be much more effective in limit-setting and getting cooperation if you avoid hostility or fear. So a true father doesn't bully, shout or intimidate. Many women reading this will remember their fathers launching humiliating tirades at them: 'While you are under my roof, young lady ...' (as if we have a choice); 'You are a selfish, rude, inconsiderate, useless ...' (true, but do you have to point it out at the cost of my vulnerable self-esteem?)

Men often seem to forget – or be careless about – the fact that they are huge, loud, and that emotionally they hold all the cards. Daughters long for their dads to treat them with love, respect, kindness and even admiration and praise. So every cut from a father goes very deep.

The true dad is clear and firm. But he isn't aggressive. His underlying tone is warm, even when he is setting firm boundaries. He takes his time, and listens to his daughter's side of the story.

Of course this is far from easy. It takes a lifetime of learning. But every inch of progress is worthwhile. Imagine how it might be, to really get this right – that our daughters respect us, love us, want to earn our respect, and never, ever have reason to be afraid of us.

Children can be happy without their father, but they will always feel this lack as a gap in their life

The absent father

Cora has yearned for her father all her life. He is a US soldier stationed in Germany, and he has never seen her. In her imagination she has found her father, but in reality it has proved impossible. Children can be happy without their father, but of course something will always be lacking. Cora says, 'There is a permanent gap in your autobiography.'

Adopted children who, as adults, search for their biological mother and/or father express this kind of feeling too. In recent times, more and more people believe that children who are adopted have a right to know their biological parents. Whatever the circumstances in individual cases, not knowing your biological mother and/or father is very painful, and can hinder the formation of a self-confident identity.

Fate always goes its own way, and children generally make the best out of their circumstances and talents. If a girl has to be raised without her father, it's important that she has other male role model figures in her life – her grand-father, a neighbour, a teacher or sports coach, for instance. These relationships must be entered into voluntarily; sometimes they just develop spontaneously. Such a role model might be found in the very committed father of a girlfriend, a male childcare worker in the centre she goes to, or a good male teacher at school.

A new man on the scene

If you, as a mother, fall in love with another man and enter a new relationship, you might get lucky and find that your daughter warms to him fairly quickly. Assuming he wants to, he may also be able to take on a fathering role. But it's important that you never try to pretend that this man is your daughter's father. Ideally, he will become a good friend of your daughter's and will have some parenting duties. If this scenario arises while your daughter is still very young, the 'stepfather' may take on more of a fathering role than if your daughter is, say, 13 – especially if she lacks regular contact with her biological father. Of course, in such a situation there must be new rules about living together – made by everyone concerned, together – and it's important to reach agreements that everyone can accept. With respect to your daughter's reaction to your new partner, just remember that friendship, respect and love cannot be forced. That applies to everyone in the house. What you should expect, however, is respect between your partner and your daughter – and the adult should always set the example in this.

Recently, a desperate mother wrote to me complaining that her twelve-year-old daughter is stubborn, selfish and lacking any kind of empathy. The daugher is turning a 'cold shoulder' to the mother's new partner. But what should this girl do? Be happy that her mother is newly in love? Show empathy for a man who is not her father? If she can do these things, great – but don't expect them. Don't try to rush these things or to enforce them.

For most children, a new partnership is a problem. But because they want to protect their mother or father, they may not say so. You can help your child deal with this kind of new situation if you remember the following:

- Even after a separation/divorce, your daughter's parents are still her parents – regardless of whether or not the two of you get on.
- Every child has the right to love both her father and her mother, and to learn from you both. If the child is still very young, the parents should determine who the child will live with and what arrangements will be made to make sure the child sees the non-custodial parent (if there is one). The major criterion here should always be the best interests of the child.
- The disagreements that parents have with each other usually have nothing to do with the children. Children must not be used as spies or as substitute partners. If you, as mother or father, feel that you were wronged in the relationship, or that your children have not heard both sides of the story about the relationship, write down your side of it, and give it to your children to read when you think they are old enough to understand it.

When girls lose their mothers

When a mother leaves the family after a separation or divorce, or dies, the children in the family are left in a very difficult situation. While the little boy loses his first great love, the little girl loses not only her first great love, but also the person she identifies most with.

'What am I supposed to do?' despairing fathers have asked me. My answer: grieve. The loss of a partner is always painful, and if you aren't allowed to be sad about it, it's unbearable. The fact that some men find it hard to express feelings like grief and fear can confuse children, and little girls especially. So if you have suffered such a loss, talk to your little girl about your feelings – show her that you are not helpless and that you can deal with feelings.

If you have joined a support group of some kind and can talk about your loss there, you may find that it's not just you who is being helped by this – your daughter may be helped by it too. And remember, there are picture books and children's books that deal with separation and death. Read these books together. Cry together. Hang a photo of your daughter's mother up somewhere, even if you are angry with her (in the case of a divorce). Your daughter is her daughter too, and it's important for her to be able to hold her mother in high regard. Don't bad-mouth the mother of your daughter; if you talk about her, focus on the good memories and experiences. As parents, you two will always be connected, no matter where your path as partners may lead you.

If your daughter's mother has died, you ought to regularly visit the grave with your daughter. I think it's a serious error not to take children to burials: this is where everyone says their farewells. There will be crying, but why shouldn't children see that adults grieve? For some children, hearing that the body returns to dust, out of which we are made, but the soul is safely with God, will bring a little peace.

In many cultures, the mourning period lasts a year. If, after some time, you fall in love again, then good luck to you. Hopefully your child(ren) will also enjoy your new partnership.

Brothers and sisters

There's an old saying that has a lot of truth in it: 'Brothers and sisters are like the salt in your soup – they are the spice of your life.' Brothers and sisters mould each other throughout their lives – independently of the influence of their parents. While this is one of the eternal truths of family life, the way in which this moulding occurs may be undergoing a change as families continue to shrink in size. Whereas in previous generations it was quite common to have two, three or even four siblings, in Australia today, the average number of children per family is not even 1.5,[3] and the decision to have a second child is usually made after the birth of the first. So the majority of young children now have just one sibling with whom they experience all the intense joys and sorrows of growing up. And many other children have no siblings at all.

The only child

There is now considerable research telling us that only children do not have the quirks that were ascribed to them years ago: they are not necessarily spoiled, precocious or socially incompetent, for example.[4] Part of this is because children nowadays have many more opportunities than previously to spend time in a group setting and to get to know other children and their families. A child needn't have brothers and sisters in order to function well socially.

Birth order

Let's assume your first child is a girl. If a second child is born, the life of this girl changes irrevocably. If the second baby is another girl, there is quite a risk that the two will compete with each other, especially if the gap between them is less than three years. Same-sex children believe they have to distinguish themselves from each other in the eyes of their parents, and most of them slip automatically into different roles.

If the first child is 'the sensible one', it will be hard for the second one to also be sensible, or to push this quality to the forefront. So she will instead become 'the sweet one', or 'the bookish one', or 'the cheeky one', or 'the sporty one'. Such role allocations are extremely common, and no-one can withdraw from them completely. However, if it becomes clear to you as parents that you have assigned a particular role to your first daughter, you can minimise the possible damage by making sure you don't reinforce it, and being careful with how you respond to the role(s) you see your second child taking on.

The oldest children are always 'the big ones', the ones expected to be more grown-up – they cannot escape this role. The oldest girl also often slips into the role of baby-sitter or 'Mum's helper'. 'It has been shown that younger brothers and, especially, sisters will turn to an older sibling with requests for help, comfort or attention if the older one is a girl; this finding applies particularly to sisters.[5] In general, older sisters are friendlier and care more about younger siblings than older brothers do.' That may be all right for a while, and fill the oldest child with pride – but in the long run this role is taxing, as it involves a level of responsibility that rightly belongs to the parents. Even oldest children are children, and like to be spoiled occasionally!

Birth order characteristics[6]

The influence of birth order – or age position in the family – is generally considered to influence personality characteristics, although the descriptions given below must not be considered as absolute truths.

Oldest children develop a set of oldest child characteristics. They are likely to be responsible, nurturing, leaders, critical, serious, bossy, independent, controlling, high achievers, self-disciplined.

Middle children tend to be somewhat confused about their identity, lower achievers, followers, competitive, lacking in confidence, quiet, shy, good negotiators. They can also have the impression that they are treated unfairly.

Youngest children are likely to be playful, irresponsible, undisciplined, dependent, troubled by feelings of inadequacy, adventurous, friendly, creative.

Only children tend to be self-sufficient, independent, loners, high achievers, selfish, intolerant, serious.

It is said that when seven years separate a child from the next child (older or younger), the environmental influences are considered to be similar to those for an only child.

We need to think of birth order characteristics in a general sense, and not take them too literally. However, similar personality characteristics that are consistent with respect to birth order have been found in adults and children and help us understand why we are the way we are. These characteristics are usually with us for life.

Mummy's boy and Daddy's girl

In many two-child families where there is one daughter and one son, the daughter is 'Daddy's girl' and the son is 'Mummy's boy'. You cannot get rid of certain roles, dynamics or sympathies completely, but beware that this labelling and subdivision does not become too strong or too fixed. One of the key rules for living together in a family is, as mentioned, that the generation gap should not be crossed – that is, parents are always parents, children are always children. When mother and son team up against father and daughter (or vice versa), for example, nothing good will come of it. Parents should support each other in their important role as parents, and if at all possible, present a united front to the children. A cross-generational alignment will make this very difficult, and will more likely lead to one parent undermining the other out of a sense of allegiance to a particular child. And it is not a huge leap from this sense of allegiance to a situation where a parent has a favourite child, which again is a recipe for trouble. If you find such divisions emerging in your family, make a conscious effort to break this pattern by deliberately doing something alone with the child who is not 'on your side'. Go out together and do one of her favourite things – just the two of you. Or sit longer at her bedside in the evenings and talk. This child needs you, too.

Different gender sequences

Parents with two daughters will be glad to discover that the two will probably play together very happily quite often, which means relatively low levels of noise and trouble. A boy and a girl do not, as a rule, play so well together.

If you allow each child to unfold his or her own individuality, and you accept each one the way they are, the arguments between brothers and sisters will also stay within reasonable levels.

All girls

If there are three or more girls in a family, and no boys, it's likely that one of the girls will take on the role of a boy. This child will develop a number of masculine qualities, because she'll unconsciously make efforts to replace the nonexistent son. If you are disappointed at not having had a son, it is better to discuss this with your children when they are at an appropriate age than to either say nothing about it or continually complain about this 'lack'. Say, for example, 'Yes, we would have liked a son as well. But we've got healthy daughters and that's fine. None of you has to play at being the boy. You are all wonderful just as you are.'

Children sense the feelings of their parents very keenly, and often try to do right by them, even if it does not always look or feel like it to their parents.

Girl then boy

If your second child is a boy, your daughter will be able to observe and grow familiar with the masculine from childhood, which is likely to give her a fuller understanding of males. The way you respond to this male child will affect your daughter. For example, if he is favoured over her – clearly, for everyone to see – or is everybody's darling (and there are such children), your daughter will find it hard to stand by her femininity.

However, if you treat both children well, so that they both know they are loved and acknowledged, your family life will be harmonious. There will still be many conflicts, of course, but they will be able to be resolved, because the basic requirements are there.

In every problem, there's a gift to be discovered

Boy then girl

Conversely, if you have a son first and then a daughter, the latter will enjoy all the benefits – and the trials – of having a big brother. And again, this dynamic can be quite harmonious, but only if this son has a recognised position in the family and doesn't have to struggle for his parents' love.

Jealousy is an understandable and justifiable feeling. It's not a good idea to suppress it; it's best to speak about it openly. If, for example, your son is allowed to feel jealous and you comfort him about it, he needn't annoy his little sister secretly. You could say, 'I know it's hard for you. I had a lot of time for you before, but now I have to also look after your little sister. I understand that you are sometimes jealous. That's quite normal. But you know, you are really special to me: only you have such beautiful brown eyes, and only you can run so fast. You are quite different from your sister and I love both of you in a special way, very much. The same way you love both Mum and Dad.'

If you treat each child with attention and respect and value their individual qualities, they will learn a lot from each other and profit from their sibling relationships throughout their lives.

Breaking the cycle of misery

The following true story clearly shows how conflict can be handed down from one generation to the next until someone becomes aware of the problem and solves it:

A mother has two sons. When she is pregnant with her third child, she visits an astrologer. The astrologer advises the woman against having this child, because she says that after its arrival, the father will leave. The woman bears a healthy girl and the father dies the same year as a result of complications after what should have been a simple operation. The woman is beside herself with grief – and dirt poor because the family has lost its breadwinner. She has to go to work, and the little girl is left at home in the care of her brothers.

The girl loves her brothers, misses her father, and suffers under her overstrained, overworked and hate-filled mother, who abuses her physically and emotionally. She grows up, but now it is wartime, and both her brothers die. As a woman, she searches for a long time for a husband who resembles her brothers. She finds him and marries him. She has a daughter, whom she abuses as she was abused. The relationship between mother and daughter in this generation is poisoned, as before, by the mother's deep hatred.

But this time, when the daughter grows up there is peace, not war, and her family is no longer poor. The daughter is able to understand and come to terms with her relationship with her mother. She chooses a healing occupation and begins therapy. Eventually, the painful cycle is broken.

If you already have several sons, and then a daughter comes along as the baby of the family, she will always be something special. But of course that doesn't mean that she should be favoured over her brothers or treated better. For an interesting slant on this set-up, read the Grimm Brothers' fairytale, 'The Twelve Brothers'. In the reverse situation, the same also applies: if you already have many daughters, a son following will be someone special.

It is important for parents to realise that we can never have everything in their life under control. Good and bad luck, and all sorts of external circumstances, play a part. That is why I cannot find an answer to many of the questions put to me. There are some difficult questions that follow people for a long time, causing many headaches:

- When should we plan a second child?
- Does it harm our daughter that her brother is handicapped?
- We already have three daughters, and I would so like to have a son! How can I handle this?

But instead of worrying about these sorts of issues, it is more sensible to look for the gift or the lesson contained in every problem. Things are the way they are – but what you make of them is entirely up to you.

In a nutshell

- Mother–daughter relationships are sometimes troubled, but can improve if the mother deals with whatever baggage she is still carrying from her youth.
- Tell your daughter about her ancestors, especially the women – they can be a source of great strength to her.
- Her father is usually the first man in a girl's life, and so becomes the standard against which she will measure all future men. Don't undervalue this vital relationship.
- Siblings and birth order play a crucial role in a girl's development.

Following in my footsteps – or not!

It happens that my younger daughter, Katie, looks just like the me of a generation ago, so I often make the mistake of thinking she is just like me. And my elder girl, Allie, looks very much like her dad's side of the family, so I sometimes make the mistake of thinking she shares their characteristics. But here's the thing, and they let me know it every day: they are their own small females, forging their own lives.

For example, when I was young and on my own I went travelling in Asia. While in Bali, I studied gamelan, the percussive orchestral music played there. When I returned home, I found a gamelan group near where I was living, and we played and practised and performed together for more than a year, and it was as much fun as I've ever had.

Imagine my delight when, after getting married, having the two girls and settling down, I found a school for Allie that not only had a progressive philosophy and a creative curriculum, but also a real set of gamelan instruments, hand-carved in Bali, in the basement. I couldn't wait for Allie to get involved with the gamelan group, and whenever I got a chance to show off my ability for her and her classmates, I did. Only problem was, she wasn't interested in gamelan. She liked the glittery costumes the dancers wore, but she said all the loud banging hurt her ears.

And Katie, who I like to think of as my mini-me, is also showing signs of wanting to strike out on her own, dismissing my suggestions for choices in clothing, footwear, and music with a blithe disregard for all my life's experience and, dare I say, coolness. I've spent over fifty years cultivating great tastes in everything, and my girls turn their backs on all that, and get on with their own – sometimes, I think, ludicrous – choices. I'm alternately alarmed and encouraged. But … so long as I get one of those radiant, conspiratorial smiles every once in a long while, I can be happy. I reckon I'd better be, because they're not looking back.

Mindy

Parents sometimes need a bit of help

Not too long ago, my wife and I were concerned about all the arguing going on between our two daughters, Jenny (11) and Lisa (8). Jenny is a caring person but, like any older sibling, can make critical comments about Lisa's competency. Lisa is a very sensitive and emotionally passionate girl, and takes these criticisms completely to heart. Lisa is in fact very competent, but she has extremely high standards for herself, and can get self-critical.

So we went to see a family therapist, and were told that, despite our concerns, our problem rated pretty low on the scale of family dramas, which was good to hear. We now hold regular family meetings where we can all air our grievances and discuss how the arguing in particular and things in general are going. It's not like we had a crisis on our hands, but sometimes an informed outside perspective can be invaluable as a source of both help and peace of mind.

Mike

Epilogue

My daughter has now almost grown up. When I think back to the day of her birth and follow the path of her life, a reverent astonishment overcomes me. When I look back on our life together, I rediscover the uniqueness she brought with her, which is still unfolding today.

Our relationship was very close in her early years. For the whole of her first year I did not work – and I really enjoyed being 'just' a mother. This time-out was made possible by a girlfriend of mine who supported me financially. I shall be forever grateful to her for this.

After this, my daughter went to a family daycare centre, where there was a small group of other children. She liked being there, and our relationship also 'clicked' during this time. I was still nursing her, especially at night.

Until she was school age, my daughter did not sleep through the night, and she needed someone with her when she was going to sleep. She had a good relationship with her grandmother, who was able to help her with this – which allowed me to return to work. Some neighbours of mine prophesised that this 'spoiled child' would never be independent. Still sucking on mother's breast at the age of three! But I couldn't have acted any other way – I had to follow my feelings.

At the age of three, she went to preschool. She still has many beautiful memories from there – plus a colourful silk cushion and a tattered photo album, her farewell present. She also made her first friends there.

I have argued with my daughter since she took her first steps. I can still remember how she came at me with clenched fists once when the ice-cream shop we were going to was closed! Yet we both always knew – and we still know today – that we can never be really angry with each other. Despite the differences between us, our connection is simply too deep.

When my daughter was four, we moved to the country. Much was different there, and better – particularly for my daughter. Living with animals and nature delighted her. At first she refused to go to the local preschool – and when I accompanied her there, I had to agree. So she stayed home with me and played alone while I worked. Later, when a new principal took over the preschool and things there changed for the better, she went there happily.

At this age, my daughter was extremely untidy. Her room was complete chaos! For some years now, though, she has had a very pretty, self-decorated, tidy bedroom – she even tidies up her girlfriends' wardrobes and make-up bags and cleans our house for pocket money. My sons do this too, by the way.

At the age of six, my daughter painted her bicycle, on her own! Until her tenth birthday I often sat at her bedside and sang lullabies because she wanted me so much.

I think the feeling of security she derived from this has given her a lot of self-confidence as she has grown. During the next few years, I played a mainly supporting role as mother. She expressed this symbolically by becoming a very confident and skilful horse-rider.

My daughter is nearly seventeen today. She is very independent by nature and wants to travel widely. At first I was horrified: none of her brothers became independent so early, and no-one predicted that she would. But that's the way it is. And I will let her go!

Notes

Introduction

1 Bartoshuck, L. M. and Beauchamp, G. K., 'Chemical Senses', *Annual Review of Psychology* (1994), 45:419–49.

1. Why girls are different

1 Private correspondence with the author.
2 Gilbert, 2001, p. 32.
3 Pease, 2002, p. 71.
4 Ibid., p. 70.

3. Her early years

1 Pease, 2002, p. 69.
2 Ibid., p. 73.
3 Gilbert, pp. 38–43.
4 Ibid., p 47.
5 Quoted at http://www.homepage.psy.utexas.edu/homepage/faculty/Langlois/chap12.doc
6 Ibid.
7 Biddulph, 1998, p. 113.

4. Her emotional world

1 Quoted in Marone, 1987, p. 177.
2 Kagan, 1994, p. 54.
3 Kässmann, 2001, p. 137.
4 Marone, 1998, p. 38.
5 Stolle, 2002, p. 146.

5. How society conditions girls

1 Focks, 2001, p. 66.
2 Tannen, 1991, p. 47.
3 Marone, 2002, p. 158.
4 Ibid., p. 159.
5 Ibid., p. 163.

6. Schools and learning

1 Reproduced from *Girls' Talk* by Maria Palotta-Chiarolli, Finch Publishing, Sydney, 1998, pp. 129–31.
2 Gilbert, 2001, p. 184.
3 Ibid., p. 189.
4 Quoted at http://www.cccd.edu/jcordova/IOWMENews 15_2.htm

7. Becoming a young woman

1 Kast, 2002, p. 169.
2 Paul B. Kalpowitz *et al.*, 'Early onset of puberty in girls', *Pediatrics*, August 2001. Found at http://articles.findarticles.com/p/articles/mi_m0950/is_2_208/ai_77480739
3 Stolle, 2002, p. 144.
4 Ibid., p 145.
5 Dr Quinlivan's study was reported by Amanda Dunn in the *Sydney Morning Herald*, 21/6/04. It appears in full in the *Australian and New Zealand Journal of Psychiatry*, June 2004.
6 Stolle, 2002, p. 130ff.

7 Kässmann, 2001, p. 154.

8 Quoted in Stolle, 2002, p. 78.

9 Diagnostic and Statistical Manual of Mental Disorders –
Fourth Edition (DSM-IV), published by the American
Psychiatric Association, Washington D.C., 1994, the main
diagnostic reference of mental health professionals in the
US. Reproduced from *Surviving Year 12* by Michael Carr-
Gregg, Finch Publishing, Sydney, 2004.

10 Marone, 1987, p. 180.

8. Relationships in the family

1 Krüll, 2002, p. 22.

2 The first two types are from Marone, 1987, p. 35.

3 *Australian Social Trends*, Australian Bureau of Statistics,
2003.

4 Quoted at www.Familienhandbuch.de.

5 *German Family Association* 1999, p. 247.

6 Reproduced from *Stepfamily Life* by Margaret Newman,
Finch Publishing, Sydney, 2004, p. 93.

Bibliography

Biddulph, Steve, *The Secret of Happy Children*, HarperCollins, Sydney, 1998.

Biddulph, Steve, *Raising Boys*, Finch Publishing, Sydney, 1997.

Bond, Geoff, *Natural Eating – Naturally Fit and Healthy*, beustverlag, Munich, 2001.

Brett, Doris, *Annie Stories: Helping Young Children Meet the Challenges of Growing Up*, Hale & Iremonger, Sydney, 1997.

German Family Association, *Handbook of Parent Education*, Leske and Budrich, Opladen, 1999.

Focks, Petra, *Strong Girls, Strong Boys. Manual for Gender-conscious Educational Theory*, Herder, Freiburg, 2001.

Gilbert, Susan, *Typical girls! Typical boys! Practice Manual for Gender Fair Education*, Walter, Düsseldorf, 2001.

Grabrucker, Marianne, *Typical Girls … Character Moulding in the First Three Years of Life. A Diary*, Fischer Taschenverlag, Frankfurt, 2000.

Griebel, Wilfried and Röhrbein, Ansgar, 'What does it mean to be/or become a father?' in *Handbook of Parent Education*, p. 315.

Grimm, Hans-Ulrich and Sabersky, Annette, *Open Your Mouth, Close Your Eyes. The Nutritional Guide for Parents and Children*, Droemer, Munich, 2002.

Grossmann, K.E. and Grossmann, K., 'Being a child on a South Sea island – childlike bonding from a cultural view', in Gottschalk-Batschkus, Ch.E. and Schuler (Hg.), J., *Ethnomedical Perspectives on Early Childhood*, Verlag für Wissenschaft und Bildung, Berlin, 1996, p. 283.

Hillis, Anne et al., *Yummy, Yummy, Yummy. From Mother's Milk to Children's Menu – Healthy Nutrition Tips and Tasty Recipes*, beustverlag, Munich, 1999.

Jelloun, Ben Tahar, *Racism Explained to my Daughter*, Rowohlt, Berlin, 1999.

Kabat-Zinn, Myla and Kabat-Zinn, Jon, *Growing With Children. The Practice of Paying Attention in the Family*, Arbor, Freiamt, 1997.

Kagan, Jerome, *The Nature of the Child*, Basic Books, New York, 1994.

Kahl, Reinhard, *In Praise of Mistakes*, Pädagogik-Verlag o.J., Hamburg, Video, series 1–4.

Kässmann, Margot, *Upbringing as a Challenge*, Herder, Freiburg, 2001.

Kast, Verena, *Fathers–Daughters, Mothers–Sons. Pathways to Your Own Identity from Father and Mother Complexes*, Kreuz, Stuttgart, 2002.

Krüll, Marianne, 'Mothers and daughters', *Psychology Today*, July 2002, p. 20.

Lindgren, Astrid, *Fairytales* (complete edition), Oxford University Press, 1978.

—*Madita* (complete edition), Oxford University Press, 1992.

Marone, Nicky, *How to Father a Successful Daughter*, McGraw-Hill, 1987.

—*Strong Mothers – Self-Confident Daughters: The Significance of Fathers in Upbringing*, Fischer Taschenbuch Verlag, Frankfurt, 2002.

Oakes-Ash, Rachel, *Good Girls Eat Up*, beustverlag, Munich, 2001.

Papousek, Mechthild, 'How can we foster the development of our children?' in *Handbook of Parent Education*, p. 485.

Pease, Allan and Pease, Barbara, *Why Men Don't Listen and Women Can't Read Maps*, Pease International, 2000.

—*Why Men Lie and Women Always Cry*, Pease International, 2002.

Preuschoff, Gisela, *When Girls Become Women: The Book for Daughters and Mothers*, Herder, Freiburg, 2001.

—*Small and Big Fears in Children: How Parents Can Help*, Kösel, Munich, 1998.

—*Teddy Bear and Kitty Cat: Why Children Need Animals*, PapyRossa, Munich, 1995.

Richter, Sigrun and Brügelmann, Hans, *Girls Learn Differently*, Libelle, Constance, 1994.

Schneider, Sylvia, *Nothing But Strong Girls. A Book for Parents*, Rowohlt, Reinbek, 2002.

Sher, Barbara, *Wishcraft: From a Pipe Dream to a Fulfilled Life*, Universitas, Tübingen, 2001.

Stolle, Dörte, *Developmental Crises in Girls*, Iskopress, Salzhausen, 2002.

Tannen, Deborah, *You Just Don't Understand. Women and Men in Conversation*, Random House, Sydney, 1991.

Index